Cricket's Child, 1945–1955

How I Never
Learned to Love the Bomb

Janice Saunders

Hamilton Books
A member of
The Rowman & Littlefield Publishing Group
Lanham • Boulder • New York • Toronto • Plymouth, UK

Copyright © 2008 by
Hamilton Books
4501 Forbes Boulevard
Suite 200
Lanham, Maryland 20706
Hamilton Books Acquisitions Department (301) 459-3366

Estover Road
Plymouth PL6 7PY
United Kingdom

Library of Congress Control Number: 2007943114
ISBN-13: 978-0-7618-3994-1 (paperback : alk. paper)
ISBN-10: 0-7618-3994-1 (paperback : alk. paper)

Contents

Preface

This work is designed as a supplementary text/reader for a variety of modern United States History classes, such as Modern American Social History or Modern Appalachian History. It is also appropriate for an American Studies, Social Change, or Gender course, e.g., a History of Modern American Women.

To those students born before 1950, this account may ring nostalgic. For younger and older students alike, it should serve as a learning tool. Hopefully to all readers, *Cricket's Child* offers an appealing, palpable history of the social milieu and the material circumstances of ordinary people in the mid-20th century in the United States.

While all events, place names and the names in the narrator's family are real, names of other players in the personal scenarios are fictionalized to protect privacy.

I am extremely grateful to all those folks who helped me on this project, including the invaluable, expert editorial contributions of Jennifer Rosti and Lynn Eckman; the assistance in every phase of production provided by my daughter, Jamie; the editorial and extraordinary art talents of my son, Jay, who conceived of and designed the illustration on the cover of this book; and last, but not least, the input and clarification of family history by my father, Carl Miller, my sister, Pat Gwaltney, my uncle, Bruce Hayes, and my cousins, Bob Miller and Gail Feichmeister. I am always indebted to my beloved husband, Mike, for his abundant and steadfast support.

This work is dedicated to my marvelous offspring, Jay and Jamie, and to their children and their children's children.

Janice Saunders

Prologue

An oft-time media depiction of the decade between 1945 and 1955 in the United States as halcyon tends to be more fairy tale than accurate portrayal. Humans are inclined to wax nostalgically, remembering the past as somehow more pleasant, more innocent and safer than the present. Historical context and individual reality portray a contrary version of an idealized past, however, even during the economically prosperous times in the U.S. after World War II and during the supposedly tranquil, even dull, Eisenhower era which followed close behind.

This text offers a social history, realistic and candid, of the years 1945 to 1955 within the context of a nuclear family. Beginning in 1945 when the narrator is three years old, the saga relates the experiences of a little Miller girl born in North Carolina. Although her kin reside in the foothills of the Appalachian Mountains, they are not hillbillies. They are far removed from the stereotyped image of a tattered, reclusive mountaineer family, scratching out a meager existence on the side of a mountain, trying to hide out from the revenuers. The Miller family is not impoverished, but neither are they wealthy. Instead, they represent the socioeconomic majority of the U.S. population in the mid-twentieth century, somewhere between the upper-lower and middle-middle classes. Within this overarching class category, the family falls within the parameters of a southern subculture of the mid-Atlantic States.

The decade between 1945 and 1955 was selected for focus because a) as it straddles the middle of the twentieth century, it provides a significant historical time frame for both the individual story and the national and global context; b) it includes the period immediately following the end of World War II with all the social and economic repercussions of a post-war era; and c) it foreshadows enormous social, political, economic, and technological changes of the 1960s and beyond in the United States and around the world. On the social context of mid-20th century America, author David Oshinsky synopsizes:

> Most African Americans still lived in the South where segregation was the law; blue collar jobs outnumbered the white collar ones; labor unions enjoyed their historical peak; shopping malls and motel chains did not exist; commercial television and rock 'n roll music were both in their infancy; tobacco companies placed ads in medical journals; and it cost . . . only a nickel to buy a Coke. (p. 145)

These are just some of the factors which both circumscribe and define the child's universe in this history. She witnesses abhorrent ramifications of racism. Most of the adults in her life smoke cigarettes, totally unaware of the pernicious consequences of their addictions. She cannot imagine "shopping 'til you drop" and most other affluent indulgences of the twenty-first century. What she does observe is her soldier father returning from Europe to begin his job search, ultimately choosing the world of blue collar for the high pay and generous union benefits.

The father of the pivotal character in our story not only needs a job, but like his comrades in arms in general, is also anxious to settle down and to enlarge his family. Women who worked in industry during the war, filling in for the men who were serving overseas, voluntarily or involuntarily vacate those positions after the men come home. Thousands upon thousands of these "Rosie the Riveters" resume roles as housewives and mothers, many of them buying into (literally) the prevailing American dream of the house with the picket fence, brimming with children. Consequently, the U.S. population explodes in the years after WWII, providing an ample work force for our booming postwar economy. Ex-soldiers, their wives, and the rest of the generations of the 1930s and 1940s who had suffered through the deprivations of the Great Depression and the shortages of WWII embark by the 1950s upon a nascent materialistic culture.

Nevertheless, a majority of the population in the U.S. in the late 1940s and early '50s still live in more rural than urban environments, depend on the radio and the newspaper for connection to the world beyond, own on average one car per family, enjoy cultural dominance by virtue of Caucasian heritage, maintain church membership, and receive their educations in public schools.

The late 1940s ushered in the Cold War between the U.S. and the Soviet Union and with it, an underlying anxiety for the U.S. population as a whole, the fear of a global nuclear conflagration, hence the sub-title, *How I Never Learned to Love the Bomb*. This title is a take-off on Stanley Kubrick's *Dr. Strangelove or How I Learned to Stop Worrying and Love the Bomb*, one of the most popular movies of 1964, starring Peter Sellers. Kubrick adapted his movie from Peter George's 1958 novel, *Red Alert*. The movie essentially satirizes Cold War machinations and manages to provide some comic relief to widely held, deep-seated fears of a nuclear holocaust. As clearly illustrated by the central character in "Cricket's Child" and more in keeping with George's book which is a perfectly serious and scary story, conscious and subconscious fear and anxiety stemming from "the bomb" loom ominously in the lives of individuals from the late 1940s on.

Although numerous novels have been set in the 1940s and 1950s, not enough histories chronicle the experiences of average U.S. citizens and families, not to mention children, during those two decades. In fact, most histories of any era offer too little insight into how ordinary families and individuals go about their daily lives, how they earn a living, what diseases they suffer, what they eat, wear, enjoy, believe, or fear. Albeit limited to specific geographic and socioeconomic parameters, this social history addresses a critical void in examining the past. It allows us to better understand not so much the colossal events beyond individual control, such as wars and reigns of potentates, but how the individual within a certain social context lives out these episodes, how these milestones impact upon daily life.

The account ends in 1955 when the Miller girl reaches thirteen years of age, and by that time, has been living for years in the state of Virginia. That year marks the cusp of adolescence for the child in the story and the cusp of one of the most tumultuous decades in the history of the United States. The rites of passage that occur for the young girl, for an entire generation of young people, and for the society as a whole during the 1940s and '50s only partially prepare them for what lies in store in the decade of the '60s.

Chapter One

Work and Angst, Appalachian Style

Nineteen-forty-five, the year the United States incinerated Nagasaki and Hiroshima with A-bombs. The Allied Powers finally squelched Japan's mission to spread its Shinto umbrella over the eastern world. Earlier that same year in Europe, the Nazis surrendered their maniacal ambitions for global domination. I was three, not old enough to truly comprehend the frightfulness of the era but making a start nonetheless.

My first sentience dates back to that year: my wet, urine-warmed sheets woke me nightly in my crib. My other vivid memory of those formative years consisted of the pre-bedtime ritual conducted by my mother, in which she held up my uniformed father's photo for me to kiss. At that time Dad and both his brothers were serving in WWII, each in a different theater of war. Uncle Ed saw action in the deserts of North Africa, Uncle Clarence endured the tropics of the Panama Canal, and Dad marched through western Europe. Incredibly, all three survived the war, although Dad suffered from frozen feet and what was then referred to as shell shock.[1] This shock, or battle fatigue as it was also known, manifested itself after he returned home in occasional nocturnal bouts of his crying out and trying desperately to claw his way up the bedroom wall.

Typical for so many veterans, Dad rarely talks about his war experiences. Only gradually over the years have I gleaned tidbits about his U.S. Army service. For instance, I found out that one of his duties in Germany consisted of guarding the castle of Hitler's notorious henchman, Hermann Goring.[2] While in the same country, Dad also reticently admitted a narrow escape from the enemy; thankfully a German family hid him in their house to prevent his being captured by Nazi soldiers. Whether it occurred during his refuge in that household, Dad never clarified, but he has joked once in a while that he got in trouble for fraternizing with Fraulein.

I wondered if Dad, an exceptionally handsome young man, also paid excessive attention to women in Switzerland, where he traveled to telephone my mother back in North Carolina after the Nazi surrender in 1945. Dad explained that he had wanted to call Mama from Germany but couldn't due to the vast destruction of phone lines in that war-ravaged country. Hence he obtained a leave of absence to fly via the Army Air Force to Switzerland to telephone home. While in Switzerland he not only succeeded in putting a call through to Mama but also learned to ski—with the help of a female ski instructor. His Switzerland sojourn ultimately cost him his sergeant's stripes, heretofore so diligently earned. It seems Dad missed his scheduled flight back to Germany from ski land, consequently couldn't report for duty when he was supposed to, and was, therefore, guilty of being AWOL (Absent Without Leave). Having over-stayed his allotted time in Switzerland, we suspect purposely dallying, Dad was busted to private and assigned KP duty. His military transgression and self-professed flirtations during his stint in the Army still surprise me; as we were growing up, my father always assumed a highly moral, law-abiding and strait-laced stance for us kids. He was also unfailingly punctual.

Things on the home front in our family weren't going particularly well either. My older sister, Pat, recalls Mama's crying a lot. Our mom, with a husband in imminent danger overseas, two little girls under the age of five to raise, a mother-in-law who constantly monitored her actions, and a car accident (ironically, a truck hauling car batteries ran into her) which ruined her automobile, suffered a nervous breakdown. The vagary of a "nervous breakdown" leaves me wondering what my mother's malady was, but knowing her as I do now, I can at least imagine her high anxiety level. At the time, I was privy to Mama's mental health problem only by being quietly present when my busy-body Grandmother Miller gossiped about it to my aunt. Until the last decades of the 20th century, mental illness of any kind, whether a mild neurosis or a full-blown psychosis, remained a closely guarded family secret.

To add to Mama's unhappy predicament, she lived in the fishbowl village of Cricket, an exurb of the little backwater town of North Wilkesboro, in Wilkes County in northwestern North Carolina. Wilkes County nestles on the eastern slope of the Blue Ridge Mountains, incorporated within the greater Appalachian Mountain region. Cricket lies just a few miles north of North Wilkesboro, where Mama drove for any "urban" amenities, such as shopping or movie-going. The population of North Wilkesboro through the years has typically numbered under 5,000 down- home souls, with Cricket residents tallying far fewer. Needless to say, everyone in Mama's community knew everyone else's business.

Regardless of its diminutive population, North Wilkesboro and its environs lay claim to a colorful history, dating back to the 18th century. North Wilkesboro, Wilkesboro, and Wilkes County all share the namesake of John Wilkes, the British Lord Mayor of London who valiantly supported the colonists' cause in the American Revolution. During the colonial era, in close proximity to what eventually became North Wilkesboro, stood a fort to protect settlers from Indian threats. The people who eventually settled permanently in the area (the town of North Wilkesboro became incorporated by 1891 with a population of approximately 50) also benefitted from the nearby Yadkin River, which provided them transportation, means for commerce, and rich bottomland for agriculture.[3] On the other hand, torrents of the Yadkin River in this vicinity historically wrought serious flooding problems.[4] During the Civil War, for instance, a segment of Sherman's cavalry marching through the area lost soldiers, horses, and heavy artillery because of the raging river.[5]

In the 20th century North Wilkesboro lost native sons to WWI and later to WWII. Meanwhile, its furniture factories and textile mills constituted a crucial part of its economic base. Throughout this time, the Yadkin River wreaked havoc (as noted in a later chapter, it was in the receding flood waters of the Yadkin River that my mother's baby brother drowned). For example, in 1940 the raging river outright destroyed many of the town's furniture factories and left others lying dormant under a thick layer of river mud. My Dad worked for a while at Oak Furniture, one of those North Wilkesboro factories which had been inundated. Soon after the flooding, he quit the company because he hated with a passion having to clean up the tremendous quantity of ubiquitous muck.

Not only periodic flooding but quite a few other events, as well as famous people, make for a rich history in Wilkes County. For instance, a native son of Wilkes, Tom Dula, aka Tom Dooley, continues to enjoy fame (or infamy, depending upon one's perspective). Dooley, a Confederate veteran of the Civil War, was accused of killing his fiancee and subsequently hanged.[6] Describing Dula's heinous deed, the Kingston Trio in 1958 greatly popularized the old folk song about him, "Hang Down Your Head, Tom Dooley." In addition to the musical notoriety, both a play and a couple of film versions, the first of which stars Michael Landon, have been made of Dula's story.

Wilkes County is also the adopted home of the once highly publicized Siamese twins, Chang and Eng Bunker, literally joined at the hip from birth. Even as a child I had heard the term "Siamese twins" though I didn't realize its origin. Born in Siam (Thailand) in 1811 to Chinese parents, the twins as adults settled down to earn a living as farmers in North Carolina in the 1840s. There they bought land and some slaves with money they had previously earned by displaying their rare physiognomy on international tour. In 1843 the Bunker brothers married sisters, daughters of a white minister. One brother sired ten children by his wife, the other twelve. Although historical accounts claim that the brothers were liked and respected by their immediate community (an assertion I find a little suspect given the prejudices of the 19th century), a moral issue reared its ugly head among outsiders regarding the manner in which each of the Bunker wives came to be impregnated. Chang and Eng's being attached to each other while engaging in physical connubial acts no doubt conjured up grossly sinful, appalling images in the minds of folks of that era. Regardless of any adverse public pressure, the Bunker twins left North Carolina after the Civil War because without slave labor they could no longer support their families through farming. Chang and Eng resorted once again to touring, both in the U.S. and in Europe. The Siamese twins never severed their ties to North Carolina, though, as evidenced by the fact that they are buried there, behind a Baptist Church in White Plains.[7]

In addition to the Dooley and Chang and Eng stories, one of the most exciting legacies of Wilkes County, North Wilkesboro and its adjacent sister city, Wilkesboro, lies in moonshine and stock car racing.[8] (There's no denying I'm of redneck extraction–visions of *Deliverance* dance in my head.) During and right after Prohibition (1920-1933), my home vicinity was touted as the Moonshine Capital of the World. Since first making their homes in the Appalachians, mountaineers had been producing their own corn liquor, referred to as moonshine (aka mountain dew or white lightning) because to escape detection by the law, it had to be distilled at night. From the time of our original colonies and well into the twentieth century, government tax agents, or revenuers as they were irreverently called, had always been hard pressed to uncover illegal stills, whether it was in Pennsylvania or in the dense forests and mountainous terrain of the Appalachians of North Carolina. No doubt some of my distant cousins, along with innumerable other early Americans, persisted in the home brew cottage industry for two reasons: a) it provided cheap liquor for their own consumption, and b) it served as very valuable currency in their backwoods barter system.

Mountaineers' moonshine business really grew and greatly prospered during Prohibition. To transport their outlawed but much-in-demand alcohol, our moonshiner neighbors in North Carolina needed fast cars and daredevil drivers who could skillfully maneuver the corkscrew curves of the mountains.[9] The driver/haulers, also referred to as rum runners, were viewed by the locals as "noble renegades" who played a "game of cops and corn" with the feds.[10] After all, they were trying to make a living, in most cases carrying on the family business. Hence the race car avidity among my Wilkes County compatriots and others like them up and down the Appalachian Range. The moonshining, after Prohibition and by the 1940s an activity separate from stock car racing, continued among those folks who sought to profit at the expense of the federal government.

To my knowledge no one in the Miller family ever engaged in the illegal whiskey business, but after Dad came home from the Army, he and Mom did go to stock car races in North Wilkesboro. I don't remember that they ever took us kids, however (perhaps that's at least one of the reasons, along with my aversion to loud noise, dust, and automobile engines, that I never developed a penchant for NASCAR [the National Association of Stock Car Auto Racing] entertainment). My parents' principal reason for attending the races was to raise money for the VFW, Veterans of Foreign Wars, by working concession booths.

The racing also brought a great deal of money into the economy of Dad's hometown of North Wilkesboro. Such was the case until the Speedway closed in 1996.[11] Originally dirt, the North Wilkesboro Speedway was established in 1947, four miles east of town.[12] It commands a special place of honor in the history of stock car racing as one of the first speedways for NASCAR in the United States.

The North Wilkesboro Speedway also became renowned as "The House that Junior Built," referring to Junior Johnson, who hailed from yes, you guessed it, my Wilkes County. One of the most famous racers in NASCAR history, he chalked up 50 racing wins from 1953 to 1966. Fans packed the raceway to watch this former moonshine runner show his stuff. The Johnson family had relied on illegal transportation of white lightning for their livelihood during the Depression. Furthermore, in "1948 a raid at the Johnson house resulted in the largest inland seizure of illegal whiskey in U.S. history."[13] Reportedly, Junior at the tender age of 8 or 9 began driving his father's pickup and by the age of 14 was making late-night runs to deliver bootleg from his home to various locations, such as Yadkinville. According to local lore, he routinely outran state highway patrolmen who chased him on the mountainous, dirt, back roads. But Junior's luck and skill did not always hold out; he spent 10 months in jail in Ohio for his illegal hauling. In any case, Junior Johnson became nationally known, at first not for his daredevil driving per se but because Tom Wolfe published an article about him in *Esquire* Magazine in 1965. From Wolfe's piece a movie was made, entitled *The Last American Hero* with Jeff Bridges and Valerie Perrine.[14]

Junior Johnson wasn't the only name to grace the track at North Wilkesboro. Another stock car legend, Richard Petty, from 1962 to 1981 could boast 15 wins at the Speedway. Dale Earnhardt finished in the top five 19 times and won 5 times at the track. Over the course of its history, the Winston Cup races were held in North Wilkesboro 73 times.[15] (Not to deny my background, of course, I must add that long before these events took place, I had resided for many years in what we viewed as the more sophisticated metropolis of Roanoke, Virginia.)[16]

Since the North Wilkesboro Speedway wasn't established until after WWII, my mama patently didn't attend any events there while Dad served overseas. If she had participated in any such "devilish" pastimes in Dad's absence, she most certainly would've suffered the chastisement of her uneducated, parochial, religious fundamentalist mother-in-law. (As we all are, Grandmother was a product of her time, place, and station in life.) Mrs. Miller constantly scrutinized Mama's goings and comings. One incident I remember of Mama's intrepid spirit which must have driven Grandmother crazy was when Mama went to the tiny North Wilkesboro airport and hired a little Piper Cub plane to take her up for a joy ride. I'm sure Grandmother felt it her duty to try to safeguard a soul as adventurous as my mama's. Well-informed, vivacious, extroverted Mama didn't correspond to a devout, conforming, repressed creature Grandmother might have successfully managed.

Despite her controlling personality and her basic "fire and brimstone" approach to life, Grandmother Miller possessed many admirable characteristics. In her own peculiar way she was loving and nurturing. One certainly had to admire her phenomenal Protestant work ethic. Up before dawn, she worked like the proverbial Trojan on her and Granddaddy's little dirt farm.

I remember both Grandmother and Granddaddy Miller as vigorous individuals, fortunately for them since their active farm life demanded lots of stamina. Granddaddy procured squirrel and rabbit meat for meals. He shot squirrels out of the trees and set traps for the rabbits. From Granddaddy's protein bounty, Grandmother cooked up fried squirrel or rabbit stew, all quite tasty tidbits.

On one occasion when I was staying with my grandparents, Granddaddy walked from outside into the screened-in porch off the kitchen and called me to come look at a surprise. Excitedly, I ran to see. Granddaddy carefully clutched with both hands a fluffy, brown-and-white rabbit he had caught in one of his traps. Just as he began to say, "Honey, do not touch the rabbit," I reached out for the seemingly defenseless, little critter. That long-eared rodent bit my middle finger (and to this day, I have the faint scar to prove it). Luckily, no infection ensued.

Besides hunting small wild game, Granddaddy regularly chopped firewood (of necessity because other than human exertion, wood supplied the basic source of energy on the farm) from great, long tree slabs. Far down the sloping front yard, across the dirt road that ran by their house, Granddaddy propped his slabs to cure against a majestic old oak. Near the oak stood his woodpile and his keenly sharpened axe, handily stuck in a huge old tree stump. Whenever he needed to replenish their wood supply, he jerked his axe from the stump and started chopping.

Granddaddy's chopped wood provided all the heat in his and Grandmother's vintage farmhouse (originally built in 1925). In cold weather the two warmest places in my grandparents' home were the kitchen, where Grandmother for years relied solely on her wood-fired stove, and the sitting room in the front of house. Most winter activity, save for kitchen enterprise, occurred in the sitting room, made cozy by the wood heat. There Grandmother quilted, Granddaddy smoked his pipe indoors, and visitors sat when they came to call. The rest of the rooms–the dining room, the front and back bedrooms downstairs, the one bathroom (downstairs), and the three upstairs bedrooms—were invariably chilly, sometimes downright cold. Winters in western North Carolina can be algid. When I as a small child stayed with my grandparents, Grandmother would seat me for my bath in a tin wash tub, placed in the middle of the kitchen floor, filled with kitchen stove- heated water. Just the same for multitudes of rural folks in the 1940s, Granddaddy and Grandmother couldn't afford electricity, let alone the luxury of a hot water heater.

While Granddaddy hunted and performed the essential, heavy duty of chopping wood, Grandmother shouldered most of the routine mandatory farm work. She was a dynamo. She fed the livestock, milked the cows, killed and dressed the chickens for cooking, prepared huge hot meals, cultivated a large vegetable garden, canned fruits and vegetables, churned milk into butter, and butchered hogs. She made foodstuffs from scratch, resulting in more refined items such as cottage cheese, liver pudding, biscuits, cornbread, and fried fruit pies.

She fashioned quilts from scraps of whatever sewing materials she had on hand. Many winter days I played under Grandmother's quilting frame, which almost filled her modest sitting room, while her plump, stubby fingers busily created a family heirloom. (Unfortunately many people took these artworks, also necessities for bedding, for granted; e.g., I recall how my father would offhandedly and unhesitatingly use a quilt of Grandmother's to line his pickup truck bed before he threw in wood and other rough, begrimed objects.)

Included among her various and sundry tasks, Grandmother cleaned the house and with her own dress patterns cut from old newspapers, made clothes on her Singer pedal sewing machine. Often she fabricated garments from her well-laundered chicken feed sacks. Some companies in those days packed their feed in attractively patterned, strong cotton material as a bonus to encourage farm women to buy their brand. My sister and I wore some of the feed sack dresses my Grandmother made, never once thinking it odd or unfashionable to do so. In fact, charming little designs, such as dainty flowers or tiny dogs and cats, adorned most of the colorful feed sack cloth she used for her grandchildren's clothes.

Grandmother handmade most of her own dresses too, although she owned several store bought ones for dress-up occasions such as church-going. Grandmother, barely five feet tall but built physically sturdy, dressed and behaved in ways she deemed appropriate for a mid-20th century farm wife. Unlike my modern mother, heaven forbid that Grandmother ever wear slacks or shorts, despite the fact that she undertook all kinds of athletic, dirty chores, such as digging in her garden and climbing trees to retrieve fruit. In performing all her daily, mundane chores she wore matronly, cotton, functional dresses and shoes. But when she went off the farm into town or even to walk on the dirt road to her RFD (Rural Federal Delivery) mailbox, she decked herself out in a more silky, fancy dress, usually embellished with a matching costume brooch.

Despite her stocky, rather countrified appearance, her very fair-complexioned face revealed a lovely bone structure with classic proportions and a perfect, wide smile. A handsome woman, Grandmother now and then succumbed to pride, one of those seven deadly sins she so assiduously tried to resist.

On the other hand, Grandmother religiously adhered to her prescribed roles: mother, grandparent, church-goer, seamstress, food producer and preserver, cook, laundress, upholder of community values, and, ostensibly at least, subservient spouse.

Grandmother Miller never stayed idle. In late middle age as her stamina for the more physically demanding farm chores diminished, she went into the wedding catering business with a younger, schoolteacher, woman friend. Even in her 80s, Nettie, as her peers called her, persisted in climbing trees to pick fruit. She terminated such rigorous activities only after breaking her hip from a fall. From then on she lived out her life, confined to a wheelchair, in a local nursing home. There, sanctioned by the nursing home personnel, she wheeled around daily to each resident's room and refilled his/her water pitcher. Grandmother lived to be 99.

Side-by-side, Granddaddy and Grandmother reminded one of Jack Sprat, who could eat no fat, and his wife, who could eat no lean. Granddaddy stood about five feet nine inches tall, bore a full head of raven black hair, and remained all his life thin and dark-complexioned from so much time spent laboring outdoors. As he aged, his hairline receded and the band of pale skin on his forehead widened from having worn his fedora-style hat outdoors so often. Except for visiting, funerals, and Sundays, he always donned his bib overalls. Any time he sat down for a spell he would light up his pipe and as is the case with virtually all pipe smokers, expended many little energetic hand movements in catching fire to the tobacco and getting his pipe to draw. I'll always remember him as a darling wisp of a man who walked with a slightly awkward gait. He spoke little and sometimes gruffly, not overtly revealing the soft spot he held in his heart for children, certainly for me.

I recall Granddaddy Miller's engaging in only one recreational activity besides smoking his pipe: chewing the fat with his cronies, sitting around the black, squat, pot-bellied wood stove at the (only) service station on highway 421, running from North Wilkesboro through Cricket up to Miller's Creek. It was at this Wilco service station that Granddaddy bought his cartons of Coke, the commercially baked cakes of which he was so fond, and the Dixie Cup vanilla ice cream he brought home to me. Sometimes he would take me with him to the station and buy me a Grapette soda to sip on and to entertain myself while he gabbed with the fellows.

Granddaddy's serious interest until the end of his life, of course, remained his farm. He took pride in his modest landholding. Once consisting of hundreds of acres, the Miller farm by the 1940s had diminished in size to less than 50 acres. The land had been divided by his parents among Granddaddy and his three brothers, Walter, John, and Fred. When I was a preschooler, my alcoholic Great Uncle Fred lived a reclusive life for a while in a tiny, decrepit old house stuck in the woods about a mile down the dirt road from my grandparents. He eventually moved to another North Carolina town. As Granddaddy's other brothers died or moved away, their portions of land were sold off, mainly as private home lots. I asked Grandmother one time when I was older and interested in geneologies, about her ancestral origins and how Granddaddy came by his land. Her response was, in her western Carolina, Appalachian twang, "Far's I know, we've always been 'rye cheer'."

According to my father, our heritage includes Scots, Irish, Germans, and English. I'm convinced our predecessors came to this country to escape western European debtors' prison, or, at the very least, they were among those who migrated to the states and hid out in the Appalachian Mountains to escape religious, economic, and political persecution. Regardless of my conjecture, my paternal grandparents and my dad certainly evinced a Scotch-Irish heritage of independence, sense of honor, democratic ideals, and physical endurance. Most Scotch-Irish immigrants to the U.S. in the 18th century settled along the Appalachian Mountains, right where Grandmother Miller declared her family had always lived.[17]

By mid-20th century my granddaddy numbered among multiple thousands who had experienced a dwindling of their landholdings. During the 1940s, the loss of farmlands, especially the loss of small farms altogether, accelerated. ". . . .[O]ne out of eight rural families left their family farms."[18] With a rapidly expanding industrial sector in the United States, folks endeavored to find work that was less physically grueling and that paid better than tilling the soil. In addition, farmers found it increasingly difficult to compete with the emergence of agribusiness. My Miller grandparents were always able to eke out a living with their farm because their land and house were paid for and because they raised their own food. Still, to make ends meet, my grandfather had to work for years at a furniture factory five days a week in addition to his strenuous farm chores. To supplement their income, my grandmother sold eggs and fresh produce from her garden to neighbors.

Included in the exodus from farms, multitudes of black Americans hoped to escape the blatant racist and rigid social class structure of the rural South and sought job opportunities in the midwestern and northeastern industrial regions of the country. Especially since World War I, having gained a more global perspective, many returning soldiers, black and white, were anxious to leave the confines of their parents' traditional, backbreaking farmsteads and to seek their niches elsewhere. As the old WWI song proclaimed: "How ya' gonna' keep 'um down on the farm after they've seen Paree [Paris]?" Our burgeoning industrial sector, along with the housing and educational loans granted Second World War veterans, added impetus to deserting farm life.

None of Grandmother's boys chose farm life although my Uncle Ed eventually had a home built for his family a cornfield away from his parents' house. One suspects that as the baby of the family, Uncle Ed felt a particular closeness to his mother and appreciated her help in looking after the welfare of his young wife and children. (For a variety of reasons, the practice of locating their homes in close proximity to their parents continues as the preference of some grown children in the U.S.) Having Uncle Ed's son, Bobby, my favorite male cousin, close by as a trusty companion when I stayed with Grandmother certainly pleased me. Bobby and I thoroughly enjoyed romping together through our childhood years, building makeshift forts in the woods; warding off our obnoxious nemesis, the local neighborhood sheriff's son; and hiking down to the abbreviated but enchanting waterfalls in the woods on our grandparents' property.

The property of Uncle Ed and dear, sweet Aunt Lovella differed considerably from that of my grandparents. Neither large enough nor designed for any agricultural enterprise, the former functioned solely to accommodate a single-family residence. As such, it featured an unpretentious, one-story frame house with a wrap-around front porch, perched in the middle of a modest size lot. My grandparents, on the other hand, resided on a compound.

On the Miller farmstead the salient structure was their modest asbestos-sided home. We joked that my grandparents had over the years applied so many layers of siding to their dwelling that it could double as a bomb shelter. It was patently well-insulated. A few scraggly shrubs and old-fashioned perennial flowers, such as gladiolas, grew close to the front porch that ran the length of the house. The sprawling front yard of the farmhouse sloped about a half acre before meeting the dirt road. Cars rarely drove by.

Across the road, between my grandparents' and uncle's houses, thrived a large blackberry patch. When the abundant, fat berries ripened, Grandmother would arm me with long pants and rags soaked in kerosene tied around my ankles, against the inevitable chigger attacks awaiting our ingress into the blackberry bushes. Garbed in protective clothing, she and I would go picking. With the blackberries we scavenged she baked succulent pies and set perfect jam. Huckleberries (similar to blueberries) were favorites of ours too. They grew wild on tiny bushes under the trees on the side of the road, past Uncle Ed's house. In the summer when the little green berries turned a ripe purple we delightedly stooped and gathered them for immediate consumption.

To the immediate left of my grandparents' place, the old, brown, wooden garage housed Granddaddy's Ford. Through the years he owned one Henry Ford classic model after another, always black. Everybody in Cricket recognized Granddaddy in his Ford when he tooled around, up and down the main paved road. Even when old age rendered him a hazard on the highway, he persisted in driving. When locals saw him hellbent on the road, they loudly warned drivers, "Get off the road! Mr. Miller is coming!"

Besides the garage, a number of "out' buildings served specific purposes on my grandparents' farm. They all lay in an inverted crescent pattern off to the right of the farmhouse. Closest to the house, at the bottom tip of the crescent sat the well house, where water was drawn from the well with a bucket operated by a crank. The well itself took up only the space at the front of the well house, under a porch roof. The only water piped from the well ran to the kitchen in the farmhouse. Grandmother reused dishwater and fussed at us kids if we wasted any water coming through the pipe. Dependent upon well water, my grandparents dreaded a long, dry spell in the weather because it portended great hardships. Either a deeper well had to be drilled at great cost or what precious modicum of water they managed to retrieve had to be boiled, reused, and rationed carefully.

Inside the well house Granddaddy hung their salt-cured hams. On the outside of the well house below an overhang, a grapevine with profuse foliage draped the top of three walls. The vine seasonally bore plump, sweet, green, scuppernong grapes. Grandmother used the scuppernongs to make her superbly delicious, homemade grape juice, unlike any I've seen or tasted since. Abundant pulp and mashed grape skins enhanced the juice she canned in mason jars.

In the open yard in front of the well house Grandmother painstakingly cooked up lye soap in an enormous black kettle, the ingredients boiling in the pot over an open fire. Basically, she mixed grease from hog parts with lye, a strongly alkaline substance, purchased from the store. Grandmother's production of lye soap occurred each fall, around Thanksgiving, because that's the time of year for hog butchering. This soap lasted until the next fall and served multiple purposes, from washing clothes to shampooing hair.

On the other side of the well house my grandparents had erected a corn crib to store harvested corn fodder for the chickens and pigs. Grandmother put the roof of the corn crib to further good use: she would gather apples from her apple trees behind her house, peel and slice them, and, from atop a ladder, place them singly and carefully on the roof to dehydrate. Grandmother took the apple slices down after several days of drying in full sun and stored them for later use. Her specialty for the dried apples was cooking up a batch of what I affectionately referred to as "Granddaddy pies." These were the half moon-shaped fried apple pastries Grandmother always included in Granddaddy's black metal, working man's lunch box with the rounded top. Granddaddy departed for work each day with this little box of goodies. As an adult I've taste-tested fried apple pies in various country stores; none are as delectable as Grandmother's.

Behind and between the corn crib and the well house stood the chicken house. Included in her mandatory chores, Grandmother fed the chickens and gathered eggs daily. She not only fed and raised the chickens; she, like other farm folks, killed and plucked them for cooking. When she was ready to cook chicken, typically either to fry or to make chicken and dumplings, she would select a bird, expediently chop its head off with a hatchet, then drop the bleeding carcass into a tin tub of boiling water. Soaking the body in the hot water made the plucking of the feathers much easier. I watched mesmerized and not a little repulsed by the strong odors, the decapitation, and the severed chicken's head invariably and grotesquely jerking around on its own. I somehow managed to repress the gruesome scenario, however, when I devoured her yummy, southern fried chicken.

Because of the (yet another) malodor and mud floor, the low, wooden hog pen was located at the back of all the outbuildings, a good distance from the farmhouse. My grandparents usually raised two hogs at a time and slopped them every day with food scraps in swill. The only structure not far removed from the pig pen was the outhouse. The stench of the outhouse ran in close competition with the stench of the pigpen. Before my grandparents could afford indoor plumbing, we all trekked to the outhouse when nature called during the day. At night, if necessary, or at any time if we were terribly sick, we resorted to a chamber pot indoors. As usual, it fell to Grandmother to empty any soiled chamber pots. Old newspaper scraps and corn cobs routinely sufficed for toilet paper.

Moving in a direction to the right of the crescent-shaped farm building complex, one found the barn. Extensive fenced in pasture land ran behind the barn and by the pigpen and outhouse on one side. Dense woods lay beyond the pasture on two other sides of the barn. A field fanned out from the front of the building. In one tiny corner of this field nearest the farmhouse, Grandmother cached her Irish potatoes in a hole in the ground for the winter. Some she dug out as needed for meals, and others she used to propagate a new crop of potatoes the next year.

The barn was one of my favorite places. When Grandmother went to milk the cows, she let me tag along. The barn usually sheltered one or two milk cows and, especially exciting to me, sometimes a litter of kittens hidden in the hay by the mama cat. I loved to cuddle the little furry creatures, always confined to the barn, because in keeping with a farmer tradition, my grandparents believed animals belong out-of-doors, not in the house. Grandmother evoked peals of laughter from me when she purposely squirted milk from a cow's teat in the face of one of the adult barn cats. The cat appeared both annoyed and pleased with the blast of milk. All of us critters on the farm drank the milk, unpasteurized.

Grandmother's big vegetable garden lay between the barn field and the front yard of the farmhouse. Although an impressive variety of vegetables filled the plot, they were not chosen for cultivation for gourmet appeal but for their properties of practical growth, preservation, nourishment, and for palatability to country tastes. Therefore, green beans, tomatoes, Irish and sweet potatoes, beets, pinto beans, cabbage, collard greens, onions, and corn proliferated in the garden.

Grandmother's canning of vegetables and fruits entailed great industry on her part. A slew of vegetables or fruits unfailingly ripened at the same time, impelling Grandmother to move fast to capture the freshness. For days on end it seemed she picked, washed, peeled and cut up; she frenetically cleansed and boiled (to sterilize) all sizes of mason jars and lids. The ample-sized, whistling, steaming pressure cooker she utilized for canning intimidated me. I had overheard too many stories around my grandparents' and parents' house about pressure cookers blowing up, propelling lid, pot and contents precariously all over the kitchen.

Grandmother stored all her wonderful canned goods in a walk-in, dark closet situated just off her sitting room. A saving grace for farmers during the Depression years of the 1930s, these canned goods remained a necessity for farmers with modest means in the 1940s. In the 1950s when we as out-of-town family members departed Grandmother's after a visit, she insistently bestowed upon us some of her canned produce as a going-away gift. My grandparents' adult children (and later, we grandchildren) treasured the canned food because it was home grown, delicious, and scarce. Other than the grape juice which was usually too limited in quantity to give away, we most favored Grandmother's canned green beans and her succotash of tomatoes and corn. Commercially canned foods can't compare in fresh taste to Grandmother's quality, organic, farm-canned items of yesteryear.

Besides the canning frenzies, one of my most vivid and pleasant olfactory memories from my days with Grandmother revolves around fetching the mail. The rich, humus smell emanating from the dirt road we walked to reach the rural mailbox and the fresh, aromatic pine woods on either side of that road were especially pungent after a rain. I also vividly recall the sound of Grandmother's dress-up, chunky, low heels pounding the hard-packed dirt road surface. Along with the substantially clunky heels, she wore her good quality dress. Fastidious about her dress in public, she had prepared for the occasional car or country neighbor she might encounter while hiking the mile or so to the mailbox.

Grandmother frequently walked an additional two miles beyond the mailbox on the same dirt road to check on her mother, my aged Great Grandma Vickers. My sister and I both dreaded visiting, and made fun of, Grandma Vickers' squat, little quasi-Victorian house with the gingerbread trim, sitting right alongside highway 421, not far from Granddaddy's service station hangout. (I should add, when first built, the house sat conveniently along a narrow, scarcely traveled, dirt road, not unlike Grandmother Miller's.) We thought Great Grandma a rather scary, tiny old gnome, bent over, and shriveled up. She always dressed in a black blouse and over-long black skirt. Likely as not when we visited, Grandma Vickers would be sitting on her front porch plugging snuff inside her jaw, keeping it in place until she had to spit, over the side of the porch onto her narrow strip of front lawn. Sometimes we reluctantly accompanied her to the inside of her house. There was no entry hall. One stepped directly into her bedroom right inside the front door on the left. Dark and rank, the bedroom reeked of stale air and old horsehair-stuffed furnishings. One or two calendars with pictures of pretty girls or flowers decorated the walls. On the right front of the house Grandma Vickers maintained a sacrosanct, immaculate little parlor, replete with an organ, as a memorial to her late husband and better days. She knew how to play her organ, but she never performed for us. In fact, only once was I ever allowed to enter that room, and only for a cursory glance. None of these morbid elements of my great grandma's living conditions deterred Grandmother Miller from trying to do whatever she could to make the former's life a little easier. Out of duty or out of love, I couldn't tell.

As a preschooler, life for me at Grandmother Miller's house offered quite a gamut of experiences. When my sister Pat and I stayed there together, we often perpetrated mischief. We thought Grandmother a great playmate when she occasionally joined our antics. Once when we were playing cops and robbers, she willingly took on a villainous role and for her punishment as a pretend outlaw, allowed us to tie her with the cow chain to a post. On the other hand, when we really behaved badly, she was not averse to chasing us around and eventually penning us down, literally on the floor under one of her double beds where we tried to escape reprisal. With a thin, limber sprig hastily broken off a bush, she switched vigorously at us, as best she could with her plump, truncated body barring her from a scoot under the bed. Her bantam arms could never quite reach us as we assiduously hugged the wall on the far side under the bed. One time we particularly infuriated her by designating her laying hens as German soldiers and then proceeding to throw corncobs at them. Catching us red-handed, she screamed, "You young-uns git away from those chickens or I'll whup your hides!" We traumatized the chickens so much that they didn't lay eggs for days following our war game. Grandmother was not pleased either at another time when she demanded that Pat kiss me on the cheek to make amends for some misdeed, only to discover Pat spitefully biting my chubby little cheek instead.

The downside of staying with my grandmother Miller a lot when I was little was the fear and dread she inadvertently instilled in me. In keeping with backwoods child rearing practices, Grandmother didn't hesitate to employ scare tactics, including demonology, in attempting to control my behavior. For instance, if I didn't stay on the bed upstairs and dutifully take my afternoon nap, she threatened my abduction by her infamous Tiny Bogus, the imaginary troglodyte who dwelled behind the curtained opening of the unfinished attic. Tiny Bogus loomed all too real for me. In trepidation I hardly moved an inch on the bed. According to Grandmother, there lurked an even more powerful, frightening, omnipresent monster than Tiny, however, who would punish any miscreant deeds on my part. That specter was "the devil." As a result of Grandmother's biblical teachings, not only did I grow up with a well-developed sense of conscience, "the devil" fed my fears and haunted my psyche far into adulthood.

Also disturbing to me as a child was Grandmother's periodic homage to her long-dead son, Billy. She would head to the cornfield between her house and Uncle Ed's, kneel down, pray audibly to God, and at the same volume, talk to Billy in heaven. According to the Miller family, baby brother Billy at age 11 had contracted tetanus, also known as "lockjaw," from swimming with an open wound with his brothers in a creek near their home. Ordinarily the disease organisms of tetanus live in soil and in the intestines of animals, but they can enter the human body through cuts and puncture wounds. Lockjaw is a hideous, excruciatingly painful way to die. The symptoms include the severe stiffening of the jaw and neck, and muscle spasms so severe that the body can actually bend backwards at the waist to form a v-shape. Bones can break. A rapid heart rate and spasms of the breathing muscles can lead to cardiac arrest and respiratory failure. In the 1930s when Billy died, tetanus immunization was not available.[19]

Grandmother worried me deeply too when in my presence, albeit it in hushed tones, she discussed the state of my mother's health (among other issues concerning Mama) with my Aunt Lovella. While Grandmother wholeheartedly subscribed to the principles of "little children should be seen and not heard" and "speak only when spoken to,"she obviously did not heed the adage, "little pitchers have big ears." Grandmother Miller was one of those adults who talked in front of small children as if they were invisible, as if information somehow didn't register in their minds. I suppose she assumed that children could or would somehow muddle emotionally through things. In any case, my mother suffered chronic mastoiditis. Antibiotics which could've eradicated her problem when she was a youngster had not been available to Mama. Pharmaceutical companies in the United States didn't mass produce penicillin until 1943, at which time Mama had reached twenty-three years of age.[20] What had started out as a childhood infection developed into an increasing problematic, more severe adult disease for her. Mama constantly feared, as she expressed it, the encroachment towards her brain of the bone infection behind her ear. Both she and Grandmother were convinced of Mama's imminent death. It turned out her imminent death lasted 45 more years, years of whispering, dread, and guilt feelings imparted to me and my siblings, all part of a more traditional, rural, unenlightened mode of behavior modification. For example, one Halloween Mama laid a guilt trip on Pat and me as rationale for not buying us costumes. She said too much money had to be paid out for her mastoid surgery for us to afford Halloween costumes; instead, she bought us each two-piece, red cotton jersey pajamas which could be worn as devil costumes but afterwards function very nicely as sleep wear. Pat and I didn't mind so much wearing the p.j.s for Halloween; it was Mama's ruefulness that was harder to take.

Grandmother distressed me too by taking me once or twice to tent revivals. These bastions of fundamentalist, soul-saving services included glossolalia, the yelling of hallelujahs, individuals praying aloud at will, healing through the laying of hands, the public revealing of sins, hymn singing, testifying, coming forward to accept the Lord as one's savior, and of course the passing of the collection plate. Heavy stuff for a preschooler. I took another of Grandmother's religious practices pretty seriously also. She often read from the Scriptures to me as we sat on her long front porch, either while we were swinging in her big swing or while we sat in rocking chairs and snapped beans from her garden. I listened very carefully, absorbing the formidable Biblical lessons like a sponge.

On a lighter side, Grandmother enthralled me with her renderings of fairy tales such as "The Three Little Pigs," "Goldilocks and the Three Bears," "The Little Red Hen," and " Billy Goat Gruff." She started all her stories with, "Once-t upon a time. . . . ." A gifted storyteller, Grandmother doctored her fables with different voices and great animation. Naturally her very entertaining, time-honored stories all carried a moral message.

While sleeping at night in Grandmother and Granddaddy's front bedroom, besides the loud tick tock of their old fashioned manual alarm clock, I would occasionally faintly hear the earnest exhortations of the preacher speaking at a tent meeting down in the holler: "Brothers and sisters, repent! Cleanse your mortal soul with the blood of the lamb. Accept Christ as your savior." These sensory intrusions didn't bother me unduly, though, as I snuggled cozily in the bed between my grandparents, Grandmother garbed in her long cotton gown and Granddaddy in his red long johns. They ensconced me for my own warmth and safety; unlike the tragic situations with which we are familiar today, there was never even a hint of sexual misconduct by my grandparents towards me. To our sleeping arrangement there was the added advantage that they could help me to the chamber pot if I needed to go. Last but not least, I suspect they preferred my presence as an excuse to avoid sex with each other. After I ceased staying with them, Granddaddy and Grandmother slept in separate bedrooms.

My grandparents always practiced the greatest modesty. I never saw my grandparents bathing and never, never going to the bathroom. Most of the time they took sponge baths or maybe they waited to take full baths in a tub after I went to sleep. I did, however, frequently witness my granddaddy's morning routine of washing his face, neck, and hands and then shaving from a bowl and pitcher sitting on a small table on the side porch. Whatever the nature of their bathing, my grandparents were always meticulous about cleanliness, being next to godliness and all.

While Granddaddy went through his morning toilette on the back porch, Grandmother fixed a huge country breakfast on her wood stove. (Eventually my grandparents purchased an electric stove, but the wood stove remained, sitting side-by-side with the electric one. Grandmother still preferred cooking with wood for many of her dishes.) Typically, Grandmother's farm breakfast included a meat: ham, sausage, bacon, or if it was on a Monday morning, fried chicken left over from Sunday dinner. Her biscuits were jumbo by today's standards, big enough to top with plenty of fried chicken gravy at dinner and big enough to envelop generous slices of country ham for Granddaddy's lunch box. Manual farm labor requires lots of energy and, hence, hearty food if available. Although people of quite modest means, my grandparents ate well—all-natural, abundant food they raised and prepared themselves. They consumed a lot more pork and chicken than beef. They kept cows for milk and other dairy products, not for meat.

What I wouldn't give for some of Grandmother's home-cooked food now, but as a child I wasn't much interested in "greens and yellows," nor did I begin to appreciate the value of food without additives. (Not many people of that era did.) My grandparents always encouraged me to eat more. They would say to me, "You're too skinny, child. Have some more corn bread, try this buttermilk (which I abhorred)." Granddaddy, spoiling me, augmented my diet with sugar-laden foods. He came home from work at the furniture factory more times than not with a carton of Cokes, mostly for himself, and a Dixie Cup of vanilla ice cream for me. The Cokes came in small glass bottles, six to a metal carton. As did everyone at the time, Granddaddy always returned the bottles and the carton to the store for recycling. I'm convinced that Granddaddy had become addicted years before to Coke when the formula actually had included minute amounts of cocaine. Besides his Cokes and his "store bought" layer cakes, he ate precious little quantities of nutritious food and in his late '70s succumbed to complications of pernicious anemia.

When I stayed without Pat at Grandmother and Grandfather's, I lived the life of a princess in many ways. I typically slept twelve hours a night. Almost never did anyone ask me to help with chores. When my cousin Bobby was not around to play with me and Grandmother was too busy to fool with me, I entertained myself for hours on end. One of my favorite pastimes was making a playhouse outside under a massive old oak growing between Grandmother's house and the garage. I pretended that the dirt areas between the exposed roots of the tree were rooms of my house. I furnished them with various throw-away objects such as broken dishes and small blocks of wood. Sometimes I played with tiny, metal, toy cars in the dirt, creating miniature roads, bridges, and houses. Imagination abounded.

NOTES

1. What was formerly known as shell shock or battle fatigue is now labeled post-traumatic stress disorder (PTSD).

2. Until the close of WWII, Hermann Goring enjoyed the rank of second in command to Hitler. He founded the Gestapo and also commanded the Luftwaffe. After having been sentenced to hanging for war crimes at the Nuremberg Trials of 1945-46, he committed suicide.

3. Engineers and surveyors laid out the town of North Wilkesboro, street by street, on former farmland. By 1891 an end-of-the-line depot, originally built by the Richmond-Danville Railroad running northeast from Winston Salem, serviced North Wilkesboro. The rail line greatly enhanced the transport of goods for industries of the area, such as timber and tanneries. The railroad in North Wilkesboro today is part of the Norfolk and Southern system. Underwood, 2006.

4. It's only been since the 1960s that successful flood control has been achieved.

5. Anderson, 1990.

6. In 2001, the residents of Wilkes County decided to acquit Dula of the murder of his fiancee.

7. Dreger, 19-25.

8. Originally in NASCAR racing, "stock" referred to "standard or production-type vehicle or part, not modified in any way." Howell, 234.

9. Illustrating the original close connection between moonshining and racing, the "bootlegger's turn" remains in use today to describe when the driver spins the stock car in the opposite direction. Howell, 114.

10. Howell, 117, 120-121.

11. Rights to the Speedway were bought by two different people, one from Texas and one from New Hampshire, where the races are now held.

12. The short track, only .625 of a mile, translating into 400 car revolutions to complete a race, was finally asphalted in 1957. Kay, 2003.

13. "That's Racin'," *Charlotte Observer*, 9 Oct. 1999.

14. Kay.

15. Kay.

16. After Mom and Dad moved from North Carolina to Virginia, North Wilkesboro's distinction included the innovative and very successful industries of Lowe's Home Improvement and Holly Farms Chicken, the latter now subsumed under Tyson Chicken.

17. Webb, 2004.

18. Kaledin, 24.

19. An antitoxin now exists for tetanus, and, penicillin can stem such kinds of killer infections. Even today though, it is hard to combat tetanus if the disease is fully developed.

20. Oshinsky, 90.

SUGGESTED READINGS

Anderson, J. Jay. *North Wilkesboro: the First 100 Years, 1890-1990*. Charlotte, N.C.: Delmar Co., 1990.

Bryant, Jessie Bunker. *The Connected Bunkers*. Winston-Salem: J.B.Bunker, 2001.

Dreger, Alice Domurat. *One of Us: Conjoined Twins and the Future of Normal*. Cambridge, Mass.: Harvard UP, 2004.

Higgins, Tom, and Steve Waid. *Junior Johnson: Brave in Life*. Phoenix: David Bull Pub., 1999.

Howell, Mark D. *From Moonshine to Madison Avenue: A Cultural History of the NASCAR Winston Cup Series*. Bowling Green, O.: Bowling Green State University Popular Press, 1997.

Irving, David. *Goring: a Bibliography*. New York: Morrow, 1989.

Kaledin, Eugenia. *Daily Life in the United States, 1940-1959. Shifting Worlds*. Westport, Conn.: Greenwood Press, 2000.

Kay, Patty. "Whatever Happened to North Wilkesboro." http://www.insiderracingnews.com. (12 Apr. 2003).

Leffland, Ella. *The Knight, Death and the Devil*. New York: Morrow, 1990.

Oshinsky, David M. *Polio: An American Story*. Oxford, N.Y.: Oxford UP, 2005.

Schlebecker, John T. *Whereby We Thrive: A History of American Farming, 1607-1972*. Ames, Ia.: Iowa State UP, 1975.

Slaughter, Thomas P. *The Whiskey Rebellion: Frontier Epilogue to the American Revolution*. Oxford, N.Y.: Oxford UP, 1986.

"That's Racin'." *Charlotte Observer*, 9 Oct. 1999.

Underwood, Dick. "A Brief History of North Wilkesboro." www.north-wilkesboro.com/history. (9 Feb. 2000).

Viens, Nicholas A. *Antibiotic Reactions: The Changing Faces of Disease and Medicine in America Before and After Penicillin*. Dissertation, 2003.

Wallace, Irving and Amy. *The Two: A Biography*. New York: Simon and Schuster, 1978.

Webb, James. *Born Fighting*. New York: Broadway Books, 2004.

Wise, Suzanne. *From Moonshine to Merlot: The History of North Wilkesboro Speedway as a Reflection of the Growth of NASCAR*. Boone, N.C.: S. Wise, 2004.

Chapter Two

Growing Up in Cricket:
Murder and Mayhem

Granddaddy Miller adored me, watched over me as if I were a fragile little China doll. He forbade Grandmother to punish me corporally. Mostly she followed his dictum, but on occasion she would resort to a minimal switching. My parents, on the other hand, viewed physical punishment not only as perfectly normal but as gratifying if we had sufficiently provoked their anger. When Dad lost his temper over one of his children's infractions, he took his leather belt to the guilty party with little compunction. Our anticipation of the pain began from the moment he started removing the belt from his pants. Mama sometimes instigated the dreaded laying on of Dad's belt. I'm sorry to say that she was one of those characteristically mid-20th century mothers who intentionally or not forced fathers into the stern enforcer role by threatening us kids with, "Just wait 'til your father comes home!"

But Mama's day-to-day disciplinary methods more often entailed reprimands and adages than brute force. She didn't tolerate whining. Long before the Rolling Stones ever sang it, Mama would respond to our complaints with, "You don't always get what you want," or in a similar vein, "You're old enough for your wants not to hurt you." I remember one summer day in particular when I grumbled to Mama that there was nothing to do. Busily working at one of her multiple household tasks, she quickly dismissed my grousing with, "I don't want to hear it. There's always something to do. If you're bored, that's your problem. Now go away." If we sniveled with minor injuries such as a scraped knee, her response was typically, "Don't worry about it. It'll heal before you get married." (Throughout the years these favorite retorts of Mama's have helped me put things in perspective.)

When Mama did resort to physical punishment, it ranged from a whack on the head with the hairbrush she was using to groom our hair, to a whack on the bottom. Mama whipped us much more often than Daddy did but with much less conviction. Adding the proverbial insult to injury, she frequently commanded my older sister and me to go outside to the nearest bushes and break off our own switches. After she lashed us, unbeknownst to my sister, she sometimes took me into the bathroom, shut the door and hugged me, expressing her regret at having physically hurt me. She apparently felt greater remorse for switching me than Pat. As the older sister, Pat was stereotypically burdened with the responsibilities of "knowing better" and setting a good example. I, on the other hand, was typecast as the inculpable, sickly little child who not only contracted the usual childhood diseases of the time, such as the chicken pox and measles, but also battled bouts of pneumonia, a heart murmur, and once even worm infestation. I recollect, gruesomely, regurgitating a pool of worms upon the floor after Grandmother Miller made me gulp down a vomit inducer. During another dramatic episode of my frailty, my mother's father, Grandpa Church, purportedly concocted a mustard plaster for my chest, laid it on me and stood steadfast watch, thereby pulling me from the death clutches of pneumonia.

Ever the little weakling, I hemorrhaged after a "routine" tonsillectomy. In the 1940s medical doctors extracted preschoolers' tonsils as frequently as they later implanted temporary ear devices in children to prevent ear infections. Since I had repeatedly succumbed to tonsillitis, a doctor decided my tonsils had to go. The day I came home from the hospital one of mother's three sisters, Aunt Margaret, and her seven children popped in for an overnight visit, with all the accompanying pandemonium whenever her brood invaded. My favorite of those seven cousins, Jerry, and I decided it would be great fun if he took me, the invalid, for a ride in our little red wagon. Obviously not a good idea–I started hemorrhaging. Mama, undoubtedly too distracted to notice Jerry pulling me over hill and dale in the wagon, subsequently had to rush me to the hospital. The doctor promptly stopped the bleeding and removed a small blood clot from my throat. More out of fear than pain, I screamed bloody murder through the whole procedure.

Regardless of the red wagon fiasco, I adored Jerry. In fact, throughout our childhood we discussed the possibility of marrying each other when we grew up. I thought Jerry awfully cute all his life, although some of his behavior as a kid flabbergasted me. Once I witnessed his dipping the top of a banana into the sand in our sandbox and eating it; I'm sure he was just showing off for my benefit. Another time he took a doll of mine, which had a fragile, wooden head with a pair of those big, blue eyes that roll up and down, hid in the closet, and stomped the doll's head. He said afterward that he merely wanted to find out how the eyes worked. Out of earshot of adults, he also shocked my little pristine self by coming out with the words "hocky" and "dooky," his slang expressions for feces.

Having Jerry and the rest of his clan periodically wreaking havoc in her home was only one of Mama's crosses to bear. Out of the weariness of coping as best she could with us kids at home and Dad overseas, or perhaps out of financial need, or maybe even lack of mental challenge, Mama tried employment at a hosiery mill in North Wilkesboro. First she had to solve the problem of childcare. Pat attended school each day, but I could not; I was too young. In those days in rural North Carolina one had to be six years of age to start public school. Neither preschool, institutionalized day care, nor kindergarten existed in our community in the 1940s. Without alternatives, Mama decided to hire a young woman to baby-sit Pat (before and after school) and me. One morning, fairly early in Mama's hosiery mill stint, the babysitter was late coming to our house. Meanwhile, my big sister, an above average intelligent, enterprising child, dressed me in a big, floppy, farmer's straw hat and a crumpled little cotton dress, loaded me onto the school bus and dragged me with her to school. As soon as Pat and I arrived in her class, the school called Mama at work to let her know what had happened. Mortified, Mama fired the young babysitter and parked me at Grandmother Miller's for the duration of her short-lived career.

Grandmother kept me at her house Monday through Friday. Every Monday when I came to stay for the week, she surprised me what she called a new "purty" (her term for a pretty object): a toy stove, a toy frypan, an article of clothing for my baby doll, or some other item to provision my playhouse. Grandmother had created this playhouse space for me on her rustic, screened-in side porch.[1] As usual, I entertained myself for hours with these "purtys" in my own little pretend world.

Alas, neither my playhouse, tenure at Grandmother's, nor Mama's working outside the home survived for long.[2] In less than a year, out of disillusionment with factory work and frustration over childcare (after all, Pat came home from school before Mama got off from work and Mama didn't see eye-to-eye with Grandmother's child rearing practices), Mama quit her job at the mill. The three of us "women" once again settled into daily life in our apartment in Cricket, where we lived during Dad's army tour overseas (and after he returned as well).

The apartment occupied the lower basement level of a two-story brick house, rented from the Smith family across the highway. (A few years later when the former tenants left, we moved up to the second floor. Mama was pleased to escape the damp first floor because it exacerbated her chronic mastoiditis.) The floor plan of the upstairs and downstairs apartments closely matched. The living room lay across the front while a wide hallway divided the rest of the apartment into halves, with the bedrooms and bath down the left side of the house and the dining room and kitchen down the right side.

The Winthrops resided in the house to the left of ours. Since Mr. Winthrop earned his living as a haberdasher in downtown North Wilkesboro, his family enjoyed white collar social esteem among the residents of Cricket. The Winthrop's only son, Paul, the same age as I, was as mischievous and spoiled as he was handsome. He frequently spun tall tales designed to frighten me, not difficult to do when I was a small child. His canards went this way: "if you touch the moss on this well house and then go to sleep, you'll never wake up again," or, as we were tramping through the dense, dark woods to get milk from a neighbor, "Indians might pop up out from the depths of these mounds where they were buried long ago and grab you." I found his threats credible, particularly after he punched my Pat in the back with his small, open pocket knife one day while she and I were busy making mud pies at our sandbox. Pat recalls that Paul was angry because we had nastily excluded him from our sandbox play. Fortunately for Pat, the stunted knife blade didn't sink deep.[3] For a long time Pat and I fantasized about shoveling up a cow pile from the pasture which lay to the right of our side yard, disguising it with meringue as a pie, and serving it up as "just desserts" to Paul.

A group of us Cricket youngsters frequently played softball in the cow pasture. Cream puff that I was, I mostly observed from the sidelines, but my athletically gifted big sister enthusiastically participated in ball games with the boys. Once in a while she incurred injury, but to her credit, she persevered in keeping up with the big boys. In the middle of the pasture grew everybody's favorite climbing tree. About six feet off the ground the tree took a horizontal turn providing a perfect space for us kids to sit on, before it again extended upward. Some enterprising person had long ago nailed foot-wide pieces of wood for steps to climb up the trunk to the bend in the tree. Once to that point, we could sit on it and play games, e.g., pretending to ride a horse. Pat, in an effort to prevent my odious tattling on her for some misdoing, would persuade me to scamper up and sit on the tree, after which she scrambled up and threatened to push me down onto the ground if I squealed to Mama. I assured her I was no stool pigeon (at least not while she held me hostage in that tree).

Besides watching the bigger kids play ball in the cow pasture, I liked to play in the woods behind our house. The ticks infesting that thicket in warm weather eagerly latched onto my vulnerable little body. When I emerged from the woods after a rowdy game of cowboy and Indians, ticks had buried in their favorite hideaways: between my fingers, in my long pigtails, and in my ears. Mama and Daddy would then laboriously remove the critters one by one, either by pulling them out with tweezers, putting a lighted cigarette tip on the tick, or suffocating the tick with a dab of Vaseline. The de-ticking procedure was neither my parents' nor my favorite activity.

Located between our house and the woodland stood an old garage. Nobody ever parked automobiles in it; we tenants used it strictly for storage, mostly of junk. The elevated floor in the rear of the garage created a dias, a perfect stage for play-acting. Although we enacted a little improvised drama there from time to time, we weren't very enthusiastic thespians. A much more important function of the garage lay in subterfuge when our older cousin, Margaret, came from Roanoke, Virginia, to visit us. Margaret, whom we viewed as quite the big-city sophisticate, surreptitiously introduced us to smoking cigarettes. We felt quite bold in our conspiracy even as we choked on our unfiltered Camels. Despite our ostensible daring, we immediately afterward tried to cover our sin by eating either peanut butter or wild onions pulled from our backyard. Of course we hoped such culinary fare would obliterate any telltale cigarette breath. Whether our parents figured out what we'd done, I don't know, but between the nausea of inhaling cigarette smoke and the consumption of wild onions, we suffered ample punishment.

In the 1940s cigarette smoking was not only prevalent in the United States, but it was also touted as "cool." Role models for youngsters, including athletes, political figures, and parents, smoked the vile weed. Continuing into the 1950s, movie and television stars smoked on screen (and off). For example, in 1951 all the main characters on the t.v. show *I Love Lucy* smoked; James Bond smoked one cigarette after another in *Casino Royale* (1953).[4] The general public knew little or nothing about the health hazards of smoking, and the tobacco companies weren't telling. In fact, companies such as R. J. Reynolds in mid-20th century asserted in their advertising that one could derive health benefits, e.g., keeping fat off the body, from smoking.

Mama and Daddy numbered among those who smoked Camels regularly. None of my siblings or I became addicted to cigarettes, mostly because, as children will do, we viewed our parents' habit as disgusting. We beheld with disdain their dirty ashtrays throughout the house. We took note that one or the other of our parents soon rendered our new living room hassock tacky with a cigarette hole. Most of all we despised both the smoke and our parents' ashes landing on our faces in the back seat of the car, especially when we took family vacations. Whether the weather was hot or cold, my sister and I while riding in our parents' car had to endure all the annoying side effects of their cigarette dependence. In wintertime, with the windows closed we suffocated from the secondhand smoke. Summer promised no better. Like most people in the 1940s and '50s, Dad never bought a car equipped with air conditioning; if we needed to cool off, we rolled down the windows. Invariably, ashes flew out the open front windows into the open back windows by which we sat and sometimes into our eyes. A family road trip equated to a most unpleasant experience for me.

Virtually every vacation we took in the 1940s and 50s consisted of visiting our numerous relatives. After we moved to southwestern Virginia in 1950, we drove down to northwestern North Carolina where virtually all our kin lived, and slept in one of our grandparents' homes, which operated as our hub. The luxury of a motel was unknown to us. No matter which kin we visited, the only way to get to their homes from ours entailed four hours of driving, including winding over the tortuous Bent Mountain road, sometimes shrouded in fog. Between sitting in the back seat, reeling with every curve in the road, and being subjected to my parental smoking chimneys, I arrived at our destination totally green behind the gills. Rarely en route did my father pull off the road so that I could throw up. Sometimes too I suffered excruciating earaches when too much air blew into the backseat windows. But the crowning agony for us kids resulted when our recalcitrant Dad refused, despite our fervent pleas, to stop at a gas station so that we could pee.

Other than their nasty smoking habit, and I must admit that represented totally trendy behavior, my parents indulged in few vices. Mama did drink too much coffee, a pot or two a day; however, I can count on one hand the number of times I ever saw my mother or father drink an alcoholic beverage. I almost never heard either parent utter a curse word in our home. This relative lack of vices doesn't mean my parents were angels. Their behavior simply reflected conformity to the morals of the average, southern Christian family of our socioeconomic class in the mid-20th century.

My parents both graduated from high school, no small accomplishment in 1937.[5] Caught up in the American Dream romance, Daddy, the good-looking, talented basketball star, and Mama, the pretty cheerleader and track star, fell in love their senior year. They married in 1938; Daddy was 19, Mama 18. A year later my older sister was born. By that time, 1939, World War II had begun in Europe. The December 7, 1941, Japanese bombing of Pearl Harbor finally forced the declaration of war by the U.S. and ultimately clinched the drafting of all able-bodied, young American males into the armed forces. Thinking he could evade the draft, Dad took a job in war time industry with Glenn L. Martin Aircraft in Baltimore, Maryland. Even though Mama gave birth to a second child, me, in 1942, Dad's hopes for avoiding the draft were not to be. By 1943, Uncle Sam added young fathers to the total 16 million draftees.[6] That year the Army called up Dad and sent him to western Europe where he stayed until 1946.

After his service in the Army, Dad came back to Cricket and immediately found work. Businesses, encouraged to do their patriotic duty and needing personnel, promptly hired war veterans. Valuing Dad's armed services record (the AWOL evidently forgiven), his math skills, honesty, and hard-driving work ethic, the A. T. Lot Lumber Company in North Wilkesboro employed and trained him as manager.

Also right after Dad returned home, my Aunt Olivia, Mama's youngest sibling, came to live with us in our upstairs apartment in Cricket. Pretty, perky, sweet, much loved Olivia filled out our household. In the late '40s it wasn't unusual for an unmarried young woman to live chaperoned with a married sister and brother-in-law while she sought gainful employment and a husband. Besides, Mama wouldn't have dreamed of turning her sister away. Being the eldest daughter in her parents' broken family, Mama always felt quite nurturing and loyal towards her sisters and brothers.

Mother and her four living siblings (a younger brother, Lee, drowned in a flooding Yadkin River[7]) had been sent as youngsters to live with various relatives when my maternal grandmother bravely fled my grandfather. My grandmother's desertion of her husband occurred in the 1930s when divorce was considered taboo, a serious breech of morality, especially for women. But my Grandpa Church had physically abused my Grandmother Maggie Welsh Church one too many times, finally breaking her hip, when he had been drinking. Grandmother Maggie walked out the door and left her children behind. She had correctly concluded that Grandpa Church could provide better financial support for her children than she, given the abysmal job market for women, not to mention the social stigma that would dog her. Since Grandpa had to go to work each day, he placed his children with several of his siblings who resided in different, relatively rural locations in western Carolina. He sent my mother to live with his brother Jake, one of the wealthiest men in Wilkes County. Jake owned a prosperous, multi-chaired barber shop in downtown North Wilkesboro, as well as a great deal of commercially valuable land. His childless wife owned a beauty salon where Mama worked after school and summers, learning to cut, perm, and style hair. While living at Jake's, Mama finished high school in North Wilkesboro where she met Dad.

A few years later, Mama's mother, Maggie, remarried, this time to a nightclub owner residing in Middlesboro, Kentucky. Without social or financial support, she had little choice but to find another husband. No living member of my family knows or is willing to talk about why Maggie went to Kentucky in the first place or how she hooked up with the nightclub owner. In any event, much to Mama's and her siblings' sorrow and ever-lasting psychic damage, their mother's tragic life came to an even more pitiable end. Beautiful Maggie, only 35 years old, was found lying across her bed, dead from a bullet wound. To this day family members question whether she committed suicide, her husband killed her, or some unknown assailant murdered her. In any case, the circumstances of Maggie's untimely death have remained a notorious family "secret"; it is the one skeleton they most tightly keep in the closet. By having left Grandpa, no matter how justifiable her reason, Maggie was viewed as a fallen woman. Grandpa's side of the family ostracized her; she was "ex-communicated." For that generation, the enormous shame of her actions and the manner in which she died silenced them all. Mama put her own spin on the cause of Maggie's death: she always told me when I was a child that her mother had died from acute mastoiditis, in reality and psychologically interesting, Mama's own life-threatening ailment. Every Mother's Day when I was growing up I witnessed Mama's crying over her mother. I never suspected the depths of her mental torment until she finally confided to me when I was an adult that her mother's death had resulted from a gunshot wound.

Mama's baby sister, Olivia, was living with her mother and stepfather at the time of Maggie's demise. After losing her mother, Olivia was packed off to live with Maggie's relatives. Grandpa Church, in the face of irrefutable evidence to the contrary, refused to acknowledge Olivia as his child. After spending her formative years with an aunt and uncle in the backwoods of western North Carolina, Olivia made her way to the thriving little community of Cricket to live with my mother. She readily secured a clerical job and soon became engaged. Once she began receiving her own income, each payday she treated Pat and me to small gifts that we loved. She most often brought me paper dolls, portraying popular movie stars, e. g., Rita Hayworth and Katherine Grayson. I adored punching out the stiff cardboard figures and cutting out their paper clothes from the paper doll book. I would spend hours by myself dressing the dolls, talking and role playing for them.

We kids, like most in the U.S. at the time, were used to entertaining ourselves. Child rearing practices and restricted finances help explain this phenomenon. Few families were as child-centered then as they are today. Given mid-20th century values and having just endured the hardships and atrocities of WWII, American adults in general concerned themselves with more serious life issues than catering to children. Lower middle-class parents such as mine in the 1940s seldom indulged their children's "bellyaching" or let misbehaving go unpunished. The axiom "spare the rod, spoil the child" widely prevailed.

During and immediately after WWII the average parent had limited funds to spend on essentials, let alone on toys. Deprivation abounded. In 1947, for example, approximately 30% of the American population still struggled with poverty. Thousands upon thousands of these poor existed, as did my Miller grandparents, without the benefits of electricity or indoor toilets, on farms in the Appalachian region.[8] For impoverished farmers and millions of other Americans, toys were considered luxuries to be given sparingly and only on very special occasions like Christmas.

Child development happened "naturally," that is to say more or less willy nilly. Parents typically possessed little time or funds to expend on their children's physical or intellectual development. Until Dr. Spock's widely read childcare books, few people enjoyed the benefit of professional guidance in parenting.[9] That is not to say parents didn't love or instruct their children; they did what they could. In our house, Dad would on occasion pull me onto his lap and read the Sunday comics to me. Mama frequently read novels (as a matter of fact, she named me after a heroine in one of her favorite books, *Janice Meredith:A Story of the American Revolution* by Paul Leicester Ford) so I followed both her and Daddy as role models and became a dedicated reader. But our household owned no dictionary or set of encyclopedias until our teenage years. As a child I read mostly fiction, borrowed from my school library.

Neither did we own a television set in Cricket. Even by 1950, only 10% of American households did. Furthermore, 38% of the U.S. population at that time had never seen a television program of any kind.[10] So, in 1947 Pat and I were indeed fortunate to have been invited to watch *The Howdy Doody Show* (1947-60) on a t.v. set at our landlords', the Smiths', house. Though viewed on a small, black and white screen, the antics of Howdy Doody, Buffalo Bob, Princess Summer-Fall-Winter-Spring, Dilly Dally, and Clarabell Clown held us spellbound.

Of course, no home computers existed for early learners' play. The one medium we children had easy access to was radio, which assuredly expanded our world, for better or worse. My family in the evenings sometimes listened for hours to the radio, prominently placed in our living room. *Dr. Christian*, *The Shadow*, *Mr. And Mrs. North*, *The Green Hornet*, and *The Lone Ranger* ranked among our favorite radio programs. (When we moved to Virginia a few years later, Pat and I would pull up chairs and hover in front of our console radio, which took up a large space against one kitchen wall. We didn't want to miss one word of dialogue, a sound effect, or a clue.)

The other entertainment device in our home in Cricket was Mama's state-of-the-art phonograph. It played 78 rpm records. Despite our modest family income, Mama managed to collect an impressive number of recordings by popular groups and vocalists of the 1940s, for example, the Andrew Sisters, Perry Como, and Vaughan Monroe. In retrospect, I'm amazed at Mama's generosity in letting me as a small child select records, put them on to play, and listen to my heart's content. Some of my favorite songs were "Racing with the Moon," "Boogie Woogie," "'Til the End of Time," "Begin the Beguine" and "Anniversary Waltz." Sometimes for Mama's guests I would put on a show of dancing around the living room to music from the phonograph.

Mama, unlike Daddy, was always present around the house when my siblings and I were growing up. Owing at least in part to her own broken home, I think she strove to maintain a stable family, to be there when her children needed her. Also, after the war, blue and white collar classes alike aspired to the more affluent model of a stay-at-home mom and a father who "brought home the bacon."

So Mama tended to us and honed her skills in particular areas of home-making. She took particular pride in her cake-baking, earning a reputation in our neighborhood for her exceptionally delicious cakes, made from scratch with Swans Down Cake Flour. Her devil's food cake with seafoam icing and her white layer cake with caramel icing were requested for all kinds of occasions, such as birthdays, anniversaries, welcoming new neighbors, and recuperation from illness. Mama also excelled as a seamstress. She sewed darling little dresses for us. Her forte, however, could be found in the gorgeous costumes she fabricated for our school plays. Our classmates, their mothers and our teachers all oohed and aahed over Mama's extraordinary creations. The most strikingly beautiful costume she ever fashioned was for Pat when she portrayed a rose in a school production. Over long hours Mother tediously shaped and otherwise manipulated shades of pink and red crepe paper to create very life-like, intricate rose petals. Pat debuted on stage a vision of loveliness from head to toe in that gorgeous rose costume.

Mama's other great talent lay in growing flowers, and from seed at that. There was no such thing as shopping for seedlings at a greenhouse or nursery; at that time we knew of no greenhouses or nurseries open to the public anywhere near us. Even if there had been, we couldn't have afforded their plants. Mama saved seeds and bulbs from year to year from her own flowers or those of friends or bought them from farm supply stores if they were available. She loved the fragile beauty and fragrance of flowers and always grew them wherever we lived. Stately gladiolas, yellow snapdragons, fragrant marigolds, hardy pansies, tall red dahlias, and prolific petunias usually graced her flower beds. Zinnias, irises, and chrysanthemums counted among her favorites too. At our Cricket home Mama planted her large flower garden, a profusion of color and scents, in our side yard. Also enchanted by flowers myself, I sometimes landed into trouble by plucking some of Mama's most beautiful blooms and to her chagrin, those of Mama's neighbors as well. She usually apprehended me, evidence in hand, but reprimanded me surprisingly leniently under the circumstances. Perhaps she identified with the ardent pleasure I derived from gathering a bouquet of flowers.

Despite our moments of minor delinquency, our parents on the whole trusted us to behave honorably and appropriately. This extended to movie-going. During our preschool and early school years Mama sometimes on Saturdays let Pat and me go by ourselves to the ten cent kiddy show in downtown North Wilkesboro. Occasionally Mom and Dad would drop us off early evening at the movie theater to allow them a couple of hours of conviviality with their friends. Our parents didn't worry about our staying unattended at a movie in our cocooned community. Almost everyone in the audience knew everyone else; it amounted to a system of built-in chaperones. Plus we children were trained to sit quietly in the same place until our parents promptly retrieved us at the end of the show.

At the theater we delighted in watching musicals such as *On the Town* (1949) starring Gene Kelly, Frank Sinatra, Ann Miller, and Vera Ellen. But mostly we took in rip-roaring western movies. We idolized the cowboys Johnny McBrown, Hopalong Cassidy, Roy Rogers, Al "Lash" LaRue, and Gene Autrey. Dad even appeared before us once as a local hero at the movies! Following the practice during WWII of showing pictures of hometown service men (I never saw any women's photos) at the movies during the world news segment, Dad's uniformed photo flashed on the screen. Pat and I thrilled to Daddy's image and instantaneous fame, even though his was one of about a dozen revolving in a circle on the screen.

Not long after Dad came home from the war, in keeping with the demographic trend Mama gave birth (after an intervening miscarriage of a baby boy) to her third child, my sister Angela. Born in 1949, Angela and her cohorts (all those born between 1946 and 1964, 76 million in all) comprised the Baby Boomers.[11] By this time both birth rates and the economy of the United States boomed, unlike the period from the 1930s Depression up through WWII. During the Depression years, unemployment stood at a whopping 25%, and the birth rate bottomed out. However, World War II ultimately boosted the U.S. economy beyond the war years. Industry continued to flourish until by the 1950s, home ownership had greatly expanded (61% of occupied homes were privately owned), most families owned at least one car, and the number of television sets in homes had increased from 172,000 (in 1948) to 15.3 million.[12] Demobilized GIs (the nickname for soldiers in WWII, "GI" is an acronym for "government issue"), optimistic over their victory in WWII and the recipients of both housing and education benefits after the war, worked diligently towards what they perceived as a bright future. They were anxious to settle down with wives, multiple children, and homes of their own. The prospering economy made their aspirations feasible. What's more, the citizenry in general sought comfort in home and family to assuage the increasing nuclear angst of Cold War.[13] My father proved no exception. With his secure, white collar job at the lumber company, his loving wife, three children, and extended family, Dad resumed his commitments in Cricket and North Wilkesboro.

In the same year (1946) Dad came home from service, my school odyssey began. The only institution of learning in our rural community consolidated grades one through twelve into the rather large, and intimidating to one so small as I, Miller's Creek High School. (Miller's Creek no doubt takes its name after one of our distant relatives.) Miss Vannoy was my first grade teacher. Despite her Lilliputian stature and advancing age, she was a seasoned

professional who brooked no nonsense from her students. If she caught a little first grader in a fib, she literally washed her mouth out with soap. (Much
to my sadness, Miss Vannoy died in the late 1940s from complications of di-
abetes.)

While never subjected to the soap ordeal, I did commit one of my first mis-
demeanors at Miller's Creek during my tenure in Miss Vannoy's class: I
pushed a prissy little girlfriend of mine named Mary Jane into a shallow water well jutting out from the bottom of the school house wall. As befitting one
of the more prosperous families in Cricket, Mary Jane's mother dressed her
beautifully for school each day. She wore shiny patent leather shoes (coinci-
dentally of her namesake) and always a spotlessly clean, dainty little dress.
Unfortunately for Mary Jane, she teased me unmercifully one day at recess
about a little plastic pocketbook I was carrying. For some reason as a child I
abhorred teasing, and having tolerated all I could stand from Mary Jane, I
proceeded to shove her into the muddy water in the well. Shocked at my re-
action to her goading and standing soiled in the well, she began to bawl. Ter-
rified by my own action, I didn't stick around to see what retribution Miss
Vannoy had in store for me. I hightailed it down the road, half walking and
half running, several miles to my house. It was early in the day when I threw
open our front door and came upon Mama vacuuming. She was astonished to
see me at home, out of breath, bedraggled and obviously distressed. No
sooner had I arrived when Miss Vannoy popped in the door right behind me.
My classmates had promptly told Miss Vannoy what I had done so she in turn
hustled to her car and followed me home. She explained to Mama what had
happened and bundled me back into her car, back to school. To my great relief and surprise, both Mary Jane and Miss Vannoy forgave me. I suppose
they thought my fear and my frantic race home were punishment enough for
my reckless deed. Mary Jane said she couldn't understand why in the world
I had reacted so negatively to her innocent joking, claimed she meant no harm
in teasing me, and declared that she was not irreparably befouled from the
dunk in the water well. (All's well that ends in a well, I guess.)

The other unforgettable, traumatic incident for me at Miller's Creek occurred at the start of my third grade year (my second grade with Mrs. Jones
passed uneventfully). My teacher's name that year was also Vannoy, but a
Mrs. Vannoy this time, probably related by marriage to my first grade teacher.
Anyway, Mrs. Vannoy thought me a cute little moppet who could sing pretty
well. She decided it would be perfectly precious if at the first all-school assembly of the year I would open the show by going out on stage by myself
and singing, unaccompanied, "If I'd a Known You Were Comin' I'd a Baked
a Cake." I knew every word and verse of that song by heart, but when I
stepped onto center stage the day of the assembly, I took one look at the huge
audience of kids, most all of them a lot larger and older than I, and froze. The

students politely waited for me to unfreeze, but thaw I did not. Mrs. Vannoy from the sidelines prompted and encouraged me in every way she knew how, but still I stood without even blinking an eye. Finally, after much cajoling and pleading, an exasperated Mrs. Vannoy came out on stage and hauled me off.

Never one to adjust without some level of anxiety to new circumstances in life, I did not equate attending Miller's Creek High School to that piece of cake I was supposed to have warbled about in assembly. I have two other salient, somewhat negative, and quite disparate memories of that first school: the dark, odd smelling, heavily oiled wooden floors (to prevent dust allergens, I suppose, or maybe to make cleaning easier) all over the school and the biscuits served up for lunch in the cafeteria. The biscuits were so heavy that, despite the fact that I always tried to wash them down with generous quantities of milk, on one occasion I "lost" my biscuits, along with my milk, right there in the cafeteria. All in all, not an auspicious beginning to my school career.

NOTES

1. Sometimes on the porch I would watch Grandmother and Granddaddy going about their business too. As I mentioned in Ch. 1, there's where Granddaddy shaved every morning. There also he stored an ample stack of firewood for use in the kitchen and sitting room stoves. On the porch Grandmother churned milk into butter with her lovely old wooden churn. After the almost magical transformation of liquid to solid, Grandmother spooned the butter into equally lovely, old wooden butter molds to shape it for serving.

2. The hosiery mill itself lasted, however. Typical of small southern towns of that era, the economy of North Wilkesboro rested on local farming and both textile and lumber mills.

3. As much of a rascal as I perceived Paul then, when I met him later in life after we each had married, he appeared quite the decent, handsome young man.

4. Gately, 277 & 282.

5. According to a 1940 census, only one in four persons in the U.S. graduated high school.

6. Hartmann, 4 & 164.

7. Familiar with his reputation as a champion swimmer, two workers on a damaged bridge dared Mother's baby brother, Lee, to jump into the raging river to retrieve some of their dropped tools. The sixteen-year-old Lee took the dare and lost his life.

8. Kaledin, 56 & 69.

9. Dr. Benjamin Spock, having published many books on the subject, remained the child and baby care guru throughout the second half of the 20th century.

10. Kaledin, 56.

11. In the peak years of the Baby Boom, 1947 and '48, one American child was born every 8 seconds. Zeitz, 35.

12. Zeitz, 35-39.
13. Zeitz, 36.

SUGGESTED READINGS

Adler, Jerry. "The Boomer Files." *Newsweek.* (14 Nov. 2005): 52-58.

Gately, Iain. *Tobacco: A Cultural History of How an Exotic Plant Seduced Civilization.* New York: Grove Press, 2001.

Gillon, Steve M. *Boomer Nation: The Largest and Richest Generation Ever and How it Changed America.* New York: The Free Press, 2004.

Goulden, Joseph. C. *The Best Years–1945-1950.* New York: Atheneum, 1976.

Graebner, William. *The Age of Doubt: American Thought and Culture in the 940s.* Boston: Twayne Publishers, 1991.

Hartmann, Susan M. *The Home Front and Beyond: American Women in the 1940s.* Boston: Twayne Publishers, 1982.

Kaledin, Eugenia. *Daily Life in the United States, 1940-1959: Shifting Worlds.* Westport, Conn.: Greenwood Press, 2000.

Patterson, James T. *Grand Expectations: The United States, 1945-1974.* Oxford, N.Y.: Oxford UP, 1996.

Spock, Benjamin. *The Commonsense Book of Baby and Child Care.* New York: Duell, Sloan and Pearce, 1946.

Zeitz, Joshua. "Boomer Century." *American Heritage.* (Oct. 2005): 32-49.

Chapter Three

"Snug in Bed
on Grandfather's Farm"?

Mama's side of the family, the Churches, judged themselves many notches higher on the socioeconomic scale than the Millers of Cricket. Even as a youngster I sensed the Church disdain for the Millers, whom they regarded as poor dirt farmers. By contrast, Gartha, my mother's father, owned a sprawling 500-acre homestead in East Bend, North Carolina, on which he raised cattle and grew tobacco. The extent and beauty of his land holdings were quite impressive. The acreage seemed to meander forever behind his stately, old farmhouse, over verdant hill and valley pastures, across rippling streams and into deciduous forests.

Grandpa's bucolic property resembled most folks' in the farming community of East Bend. The tiny town (current population totaling 659 according to the 2000 census) derives its name from its proximity to the east bend of the Yadkin River. Located in Yadkin County and covering only 1.3 miles in area, East Bend lies seventeen miles west of Winston-Salem. The two areas couldn't be more different. Time seems to have stood still in East Bend. Originally it was called Banner's Store, after the merchant Martin Banner, who supplied wares to farm families in the region. It's believed that people started referring to the hamlet by its present name when in 1849 a U. S. Post Office designated "East Bend" opened there. Residents had the chance in 1885 to enhance development in the town by buying bonds to build a railroad; however, considering trains a nuisance, among other things for scaring cattle and necessitating more fence building, they didn't invest. (Ironically for my relatives and me, the proposed railroad would have conveniently connected East Bend to Wilkesboro.) Despite that missed opportunity, around the turn of the century East Bend thrived with two hotels and two buggy factories. Of the latter, Huff's Buggy was one of the largest of its kind in the South; alas, Huff's met its demise with the advent of automobiles. Since then businesses of various kinds and movie theaters have come and mostly gone in East Bend. Today the majority of residents of the town commute to Winston-Salem for work and for other of life's necessities.[1]

Winston-Salem certainly provided the tobacco industry, most specifically the R. J. Reynolds empire, to which Grandpa could market his crop. Aptly, the city answers to two nicknames, one of which is "Camel," obviously alluding to its famous cigarette brand. The other name, "Twin City," reflects its history. The Moravians founded Salem (meaning "peace") in 1753 as their exclusive religious community, replete with a church, other public buildings, and both a Brethrens' and a Sisters' home for unmarried congregation members. The nearby secular town of Winston, named after Joseph Winston, a hero of the Revolutionary War, originated in 1849. In 1913 Winston and Salem officially joined their towns. The early Moravian community survives today as Old Salem, an historic district of Winston-Salem. In German, the Moravians referred to their early settlement as "die Wachau," or in Latin translation, "Wachovia," the name chosen for today's bank conglomerate and headquarters in Winston-Salem. The Twin City gave birth in 1937 to yet another wildly successful brand name product, Krispy Kreme, the food value of which may be compared to, at least in the ironic sense of "quick energy" and possibly addiction, that of cigarettes.[2]

Not only Winston-Salem but the whole state of North Carolina is famous for tobacco. North Carolina ranks as one of the top two (Kentucky is the other) tobacco growing states and produces half of all the flue-cured tobacco in the U. S. Tobacco was a natural choice of crop for Grandpa Church. The Carolinas (and Virginia) have for centuries been profiting from growing tobacco, starting with the Jamestown Colony 400 years ago. Only when the colonists stumbled upon the market value of tobacco smoking were they able to save their defunct colony. Not until two centuries later, though, in 1839, did the discovery of "Bright Leaf" raise the tobacco crop to new financial heights. According to a generally accepted story, a slave named Stephen (his last name apparently never recorded) built in his master's tobacco barn a small fire for some purpose–perhaps to cook a meal for himself or simply to stay warm–and the heat from the fire cured (dried out the sap in) the tobacco leaves to a perfectly fragrant, perfectly golden-colored quality. Having thus attained an infinitely more refined, ultimately more tasty tobacco product through heat curing (rather than simply air curing), the tobacco plant truly earned its reputation as "the coin of the realm" or "The Golden Token."[3]

The invention of a cigarette machine near the end of the 19th century revolutionized the tobacco industry. But it was in the early 20th century with WWI that the cigarette market gained broad momentum. In the "Great War"

(WWI), General Pershing declared that cigarettes were as essential as bullets for the troops. Cigarettes had come to symbolize comradeship and civility in the face of the brutality of war. A soldier often shared a smoke with his comrade in arms, and sometimes he shared one with an enemy soldier during a pause in hostilities, for instance, on Christmas Day. In prison camps of WWII, cigarettes were used as currency; i.e., if a soldier possessed cigarettes, he could trade them for various other items he might need from his fellow prisoners or from prison guards. If a soldier faced a firing squad, he customarily was offered a cigarette before dying, a humanitarian gesture amid war atrocities. Whatever the case, tobacco companies happily accommodated both Pershing and our soldiers by sending millions of free cigarettes to them.[4] My Grandpa Church, a veteran of WWI, usually held a cigarette in his hand every time we visited him, which was at least once a year until I was 18 years old.

When Grandpa Church first bought his farm in the 1940s, growing tobacco was profitable. For one thing, he could avail himself of cheap labor: he hired poor white and black laborers to harvest the crop. For another, FDR during WWII decreed tobacco a war material and, hence, a protected crop. In other words, farmers could plant tobacco without fear that they would lose their investment. Finally, during World War II, because cigarettes supplied quick energy and supposedly calmed GI nerves, they were included, again without charge from the giant tobacco companies, in soldiers' rations. The individual U.S. troop tobacco allowance totaled from five to seven packs a week in WWII. GIs were so identified with certain brands of cigarettes included in their rations that a number of repatriation camps in France were named after cigarette brands, e.g., Camp Chesterfield and Camp Pall Mall. Predictably, troops returned home from WWII, just as they had from WWI, addicted, with Camels a great favorite.[5] It was in the years following WWII, however, that the market for tobacco took off most dramatically. By 1949, "44-47% of all adult Americans smoked," with men comprising the majority.[6] In that same year, tobacco farmers again profited from price supports through the renewed Agricultural Adjustment Act.

Grandpa's property stood smack dab in the middle of tobacco country, home to the R. J. Reynolds tobacco empire. Reynolds founded his legendary tobacco company in Winston in 1875 at which time he produced chewing tobacco. During the next thirty years, though, James "Buck" Duke developed a monopoly over the tobacco business and totally overshadowed the Reynolds Company. Fortunately for Reynolds, the U.S. "trust busting" of 1911 allowed him finally to compete successfully against Duke's American Tobacco Company, as well as other tobacco firms such as Philip Morris.[7]

Grandpa worked at R. J. Reynolds as a security guard in Winston-Salem when he decided to buy the farm at East Bend. He and his second wife, my step-Grandma Texie, quit their jobs at Reynolds (where they had met) and used their combined savings to buy into their dream of a lifetime. Located off a two-lane paved highway, about a mile out on a dirt road, Grandpa's farmhouse and yard were neatly encased in the front and sides by a white fence. Beyond the fenced-in yard to the left of the house lay a field belonging to the next door neighbors. To the right of the house alongside the fence grew a line of half a dozen mature mimosa trees. Those mimosa trees bloomed gloriously pink and smelled paradisiacally in the summer. Directly behind the house and a narrow lawn lay Grandma Texie's huge vegetable garden and sizeable strawberry patch. Inside the fence on the right lawn of the house stood a 20 foot or so, old, picturesque, wooden windmill which pumped water for Grandpa's house.[8] A path running between the windmill and an old storage house in the side yard led to Grandpa's back door. It was through this door, opening into the kitchen, that we always entered the house when we came to visit.

The Church farmhouse itself differed in a number of respects from that of the Millers'. Grandpa's house was centrally heated, and although there was only one bathroom, it lay claim to indoor plumbing as far back as I can recall. Grandpa's white, wood-frame, rambling homestead included four spacious rooms downstairs and two very large bedrooms upstairs. When we came for a holiday, Pat and I slept in the bedroom upstairs directly over the living room. Though our parents thought us safely tucked away in our beds for the night, on our knees we cleverly eavesdropped through the old heat grate in the middle of our bedroom floor on the adult conversation below us. Typically, though, the talk consisted mostly of tedious family gossip; we soon grew bored and crept back to bed.

Since my biological grandmother on the Church side, Maggie, had met her demise years before I was born, I knew only Grandma Texie. Although differing considerably in looks, both Maggie and Texie were beautiful women. I can judge Maggie's appearance only from photographs and from Church family lore, but Texie I saw at regular intervals when I was growing up. Tiny Maggie's face featured high cheekbones, a roses and cream complexion, big brown eyes, and a dark brown spit curl of hair strategically sculpted on her forehead. Maggie, at least in my favorite photo of her, and my mother looked very much alike. Texie, a plump woman and much more fair complexioned than Maggie, possessed a lovely face set off by her light blue eyes and a full head of white hair which she always kept permed. By the time I knew her, she had long ago lost the blush of youth.

Mama and her siblings professed to hating their stepmother Texie until they became married adults with children. My Aunt Ruby particularly loathed Texie and contended that Texie acted despicably towards her and Lee, the baby brother of the family, when they as children lived with her and Grandpa. When in her presence as adults, though, Texie's stepchildren appeared tolerant and hid any animosity they harbored. Regardless of her stepchildren's feelings, Texie never acted unkindly to me or my sisters. Just the same, we couldn't help but notice that she pursed her lips more or less continuously. I intuited, especially as I matured, that Texie herself nursed bitterness, probably because she had borne no children of her own and was continuously subjected not only to Grandpa Church's children but to his numerous grandchildren as well.

Once I accidentally glimpsed Grandma Texie partially nude as she was coming out of the shower; I thought the roll of fat hanging around her waist and down her abdomen peculiar looking. I had never before seen an elderly person in the nude, let alone a plump one. The type and quantity of food she consumed on the farm probably accounted for Texie's fleshiness. She and Grandpa regularly ate fatted beef, drank whole milk, and seasoned their food with real cream and butter. The Churches consistently sat down to a richly laden table.

Whenever our family stayed with them, we were invariably treated, among other farm gourmet goodies, to steaks carved from Grandpa's beef cattle. Grandpa and Grandma Texie stored the steaks in one of the two floor freezers sitting side-by-side against one wall of their dining room. In preparation for dinner my grandparents would take out the steaks to thaw and, when they had defrosted to room temperature, throw them in a big fry pan greased with butter and sear them on each side to tender perfection. In those same freezers, Grandma also always kept on hand her homegrown sweet strawberries, a far cry in flavor from the under-ripened, tasteless ones sold in our modern-day supermarkets; melt-in-your-mouth, fat-saturated, homemade whipped cream; and several of the plain but nonetheless delicious, moist, white cakes she made from scratch. She served us year round for dessert, extraordinarily scrumptious, fresh strawberry shortcake with whipped cream. To complement the best-ever steaks for dinner, Grandma would bring out from the root cellar under one side of the farmhouse, canned fresh vegetables to heat and serve. As did my Grandmother Miller, Texie made us happy when she gave us some of her canned goods to take back home.

Grandma Texie appeared to be devoted to Grandpa Church, despite the fact that, according to my Aunt Ruby who witnessed the altercation as a child, Grandpa in a fit of alcohol- induced anger, stopped his car on the shoulder of the road , pulled Texie out and beat her. This incident occurred during the winter; luckily for Texie, one supposes, a woolen coat somewhat cushioned the blows. During our short stays at Grandpa and Texie's I neither saw nor heard any indication of wife abuse. Of course, by the time I knew them,

Grandpa had totally ceased drinking. What I can vouch for is Texie's deference to Grandpa, in conversation, in farm work, in politics, and in financial matters. I never visited by myself for any extended period at my maternal grandparents' home so I don't really know how they related to each other in private.

Aunt Ruby's testimony notwithstanding, we grandchildren regarded Grandpa with great respect and fondness. He always related to us with kindness. Sometimes he would take one of us children on a tractor ride, or he would offer us what he considered another treat: a drink from a dipper in the bucket of fresh milk he was carrying from the barn to the farmhouse kitchen. Not to hurt Grandpa's feelings or dampen his enthusiasm, we smiled politely and dutifully swallowed the proffered, ghastly sip. Accustomed at our house to a cold, pasteurized product, we could barely manage to swallow the raw, warm milk.

Whenever our family first arrived at Grandpa's for a visit, he liked to stand, while we usually sat, in his big farm kitchen and talk at great length in his engaging southern drawl. He dominated the conversation while his adult children, their spouses, and his grandchildren all seemed perfectly content to listen. We all perceived blue-eyed, Scandinavian fair-skinned Grandpa Church as a giant of a man, knowledgeable, gentle and articulate. It amused him to lay my diminutive hand on top of his huge one and compare the sizes. Too, he always bade me sing for his delight a particular little ditty I learned in elementary school. The lyrics go as follows:

> Snug in bed on grandfather's farm,
> I hear the katydids' sounding alarm.
> Frogs and tree toads keep me awake.
> What a remarkable chorus they make.

> —Author Unknown

One of the only times I remember having Grandpa all to myself was when he let me accompany him to a cattle auction. I didn't actually see any of the auction; Grandpa left me in the parking lot of the stockyards to wait for him in the seat of his pickup truck. Although no responsible parent or grandparent would dare do this today, Grandpa believed, justifiably in that era, I would be completely safe alone in his truck. As I waited for what seemed hours with nothing for entertainment save my own lively imagination, I felt excited. I smelled the penetrating, earthy animal and hay aromas and heard the lively sounds of men talking and the skillful auctioneer plying his trade. Grandpa came once to check on me and to bring me a fried egg sandwich for lunch. Famished by that time, I thought the sandwich an exceptional treat. That was the first and last fried egg sandwich I tasted until I became an adult.

As was the case with the Miller farm, Grandpa Church's place never ceased to hold adventure for us. To begin with, Pat often purposely "lost" herself to avoid Texie. Not that Grandma Texie mistreated her; Pat just didn't like her. There were plenty of places to hide: the expansive cattle barn, the tractor garage, a couple of old equipment storehouses, and the vast yard.

One silly adventure of ours at Grandpa's involved once again our older, culpable cousin, Margaret, and her little sister, Judy. Judy was years younger than Margaret, two years younger even than I. Probably because we knew we weren't supposed to, we decided to play in Grandpa's grain storage loft atop his tractor garage. The storage area consisted simply of one small room, the floor of which was piled high, wall-to-wall, with loose wheat grain. Margaret, Pat, and I more or less sat atop the grain, watching as Judy gleefully wallowed in it, a typically puerile thing to do. Since Judy wore a dress and flimsy little underpants at the time, one can imagine her eventual discomfort from the frolic in the grain loft. As far as we knew, the grownups remained oblivious to our trespassing upon and contamination of Grandpa's wheat store.

On a rare but always wonderful Sunday afternoon my grandparents would host a Church family reunion. We all gathered in the sizeable front yard and on the large, wrap-around front porch of the house for an ice cream social. On the grass around the massive old oak trees we kids romped and played games while on the porch parents chatted and cranked the handles of the ice cream makers. If by chance we children behaved ourselves and the grownups felt patient, they would let us take a turn at cranking the handles. After what seemed an eternity, the ice cream finally set up, ready to eat. We all thought we had died and gone to heaven when we lounged in the shade and feasted on luscious, creamy vanilla and peach homemade ice cream. Only the most natural, wholesome, fatty ingredients went into that ice cream!

Grandpa was proud of his and Texie's farm and of his herd of cattle. One year as a teenager when I had started working part-time as a switchboard operator at the Chesapeake and Potomac Telephone Company, Grandpa suggested I invest in a calf which he would raise for me. As soon as possible I saved $100 for the investment and took him up on his offer. True to his word, he raised the calf and sold it for several hundred, sharing his profits with me. We were both pleased with the results of my first capital venture.

All of us grandchildren could've earned money in the summers picking tobacco for Grandpa if we had been willing, but we were not. In the 1950s tobacco was still almost all harvested by hand, a hot, arduous, labor-intensive job. Harvesting begins when the leaves on the bottom of a tobacco stalk turn yellow, indicating ripeness. Harvesting, or priming as it is called, entails working from the bottom of the stalk up, picking the large, tongue-shaped leaves one-by-one, as each leaf reaches just the right stage of maturity. Flavor is lost from a leaf if it is harvested too early. Pickers must submerge themselves among the four to six feet high stalks bearing as many as twenty leaves apiece, in intervals of about every two weeks to complete the harvesting. The first round may yield only six or so leaves per stalk. Depending upon the maturity rate of the leaves as ripeness moves from the bottom to the middle and finally to the top, it may take up to seven times over many weeks of trudging into the field to complete the harvesting.[9]

For years Grandpa grew the "golden token," but as he grew older and hired hands were no longer to be found, he rented out acreage for other farmers to grow tobacco crops. By the late 1940s and early '50s droves of hired hands, as well as small-holding farmers, had forsaken grueling farm work such as harvesting and curing tobacco in search of greater opportunities and less onerous, more lucrative jobs in urban areas. Starting about that time, Grandpa left some of his acreage fallow because the federal government paid him an annual subsidy for doing so.

The only laborer I met who still worked on Grandpa's farm when I was a child was a very elderly, wizened, sweet black man. With a hint of both mirth and love, he would sit on his haunches at my level, look seriously into my eyes and talk to me as if I was of grown up importance. He liked to predict my future. The only thing I remember about the predictions is that they invariably boded well for me. I never saw him again after I was old enough to enter school. No one thought to tell me his fate; I assumed he had died, but I never forgot his enchanting character.

Grandpa also tried to talk his children and later us grandchildren and our spouses into becoming his partners in agriculture. We weren't interested in that either. One of the main reasons neither our parents nor we were willing to commit to the farming business was the same reason we always vacationed at our grandparents' instead of vice-versa: every single day of the year, year in and year out, cattle must be fed and led to and from the pasture, cows must be milked, pigs have to be slopped, or chickens have to be fed. Nothing can wait. What's more, in case of inclement weather the farmer needs always to be available to protect crops, livestock, equipment, or buildings. Without farm workers, and completely reliable ones at that, farmers such as Grandpa couldn't abandon their work, not even for a brief respite. We were well aware of our grandparents' necessary constant vigil and were unwilling to relinquish the scheduled leisure time afforded us by our modern industrial economy. So Grandpa kept at his farm work with no one to help him but my elderly black friend early on, an occasional migrant worker, and Texie, who really wasn't physically able to perform heavy farm chores.

After I had married and started my own family, we received the news that Grandpa had suffered a stroke. He had been tending his cattle out in a pasture when he suddenly lost sight in one eye. He was rushed to the hospital where it was determined that his left carotid artery was completely blocked. Although the last thing he wanted to do, after his stroke Grandpa finally had to sell his farm and retire. Subsequently he and Texie purchased in Boonville, North Carolina, a nice ranch home, surrounded by several acres of land, enough that Grandpa could still derive pleasure from mounting his John Deere riding mower and cutting their expansive lawn. Texie could still raise and can vegetables.

NOTES

1. www.greeneggsandsam.com/eastbend (23 Jan. 2006).
2. Tursi.
3. Walls, 56-57.
4. Gately, 233-34 & 261.
5. Gately, 257 & 265.
6. Borio, 8.
7. Borio, 3.
8. In the past, windmills provided a great number of services for farms ranging from grinding grains, such as wheat, corn, and barley to make flour or meal; grinding seeds, such as mustard or lindseed; pounding hemp to make rope; to even sawing logs. And as in the case of countries such as the Netherlands, windmills have reprieved inundated land by pumping out water.
9. Gately, 367-68.

SUGGESTED READINGS

Borio, Gene. "The History of Tobacco Part III." www.historian.org/bysubject/tobacco3.htm (4 Feb. 2006).

Crews, C. Daniel, and Richard W. Starbuck. *With Courage for the Future: The Story of the Moravian Church, Southern Province.* Winston-Salem: Blair Publishing, 2002.

Gately, Iain. *Tobacco: A Cultural History of How an Exotic Plant Seduced Civilization.* New York: Grove Press, 2001.

Goodman, Jordan. *Tobacco in History and Culture.* London: Routledge, 1993.

____ . *Tobacco in History: The Cultures of Dependence.* Detroit: Charles Scriber's Sons, 2004.

Hart, John Fraser. *The Changing Scale of American Agriculture.* Charlottesville: University of Virginia Press, 2003.

Jenkins, Garry. "Wind Energy–A Brief History and Current Status." *Nutrition and Food Science* (March 1999): 157.

Larkin, David. *Mill: The History and Future of Naturally Powered Buildings.* New York: Universe, 2000.

Schlebecker, John T. *Whereby We Thrive: A History of American Farming,* 1607-1972. Ames, Ia.: Iowa State UP, 1975.

Tursi, Frank V. *Winston-Salem: A History.* Winston-Salem: Blair Publishing, 1994.

Walls, Dwayne E. *The Chickenbone Special.* New York: Harcourt Brace Jovanovich, Inc., 1971.

www.greeneggsandsam.com/eastbend. (23 Jan. 2006).

Chapter Four

Adjusting to
New Home and New Hood

In 1950 Mama's brother, Zollie, convinced Dad to come to Roanoke, a small town in southwestern Virginia, and to seek employment with the long-distance trucking firm of Associated Transport. Uncle Zollie had moved years previously from Kentucky (he had lived in Kentucky to be near his mother, Maggie, before she died) to Roanoke to work for Associated and found driving the big sleeper rigs not only agreeable but quite lucrative as well. Upon Zollie's urging, Dad applied for a job with Associated too and was hired. Dad moved to Roanoke and started work on the road. Having decided that both the truck driving and the salary suited him well, Dad made arrangements for us to join him.[1]

When Dad informed us that we were moving away from the only home I had ever known to relocate near Tenth Street in a strange town, I began to worry. I agonized over the prospect of leaving my pals, my extended family members, and my school. Also, the only Tenth Street familiar to me was a main thoroughfare in downtown North Wilkesboro, characterized by a bustling, sometimes seedy population, any one of whom might whisk me away. Or at least, that's what Grandmother Miller convinced me of as she and I walked down Tenth Street whenever she had business in North Wilkesboro. As she tightly held my hand, she emphatically warned me of the dangers of taking candy from strangers.

Although Grandmother Miller bemoaned our move, my immediate family had no problem with it. Mama had always felt socially and intellectually cramped in the 1940s provincialism of Miller's Creek, Cricket, and North Wilkesboro. My older sister, Pat, invariably more stoical and practical than I, expressed little concern about either our new location or our new school. Newly born, sister Angela knew no difference. With a family of five to support, Dad jumped at the chance for upward economic mobility. With Associated he earned a much higher income than he had made as a lumber company manager. Plus, he joined the Teamsters, paid his union dues, and derived excellent benefits from that organization.[2]

I was the only one who died the proverbial one thousand deaths in anticipation of our move, only to find out that our new address was actually Howbert Avenue, a good distance from Tenth Street in Roanoke. (Besides, Tenth Street in Roanoke has never crawled with predators, as I had imagined.) Howbert Avenue in the 1950s offered a welcoming, shady street in a comfortable, predominantly middle-class (lower-middle and middle-middle, to be more precise) neighborhood, populated with children of all ages. Our family, including Pat, age 10 ½, I at 8 years of age, and baby Angela fitted right in.

We first lived on Howbert in a rented upstairs apartment of a charming old, two-storied house. To enter the apartment, we came through our landlady's, Mrs. Persinger's, front door, crossed her foyer, where lace-curtained French doors afforded her privacy in her own downstairs apartment, and proceeded up the staircase to the left.

The screened-in back porch of our little apartment stands out most in my mind, perhaps because it opened up the otherwise cramped accommodations of our four rooms and a bath. In the summertime on that porch, we often ate a light supper of green beans, boiled potatoes with butter, sliced homegrown tomatoes, and corn bread, always washed down with sweetened, home brewed iced tea. If we were lucky, we might catch a soft summer breeze while we delighted in a dessert of succulent, locally grown cantaloupe halves, scooped out and filled with Neopolitan ice cream.

Mrs. Persinger, a widow, seemed quite elderly to me then but probably was only in her 60's. A bit prissy in her mannerisms and always impeccably attired in dress and heels, she personified the Southern Lady. Mrs. Persinger wanted to befriend us children, but her constant teasing mortified me. I don't remember that she teased my siblings. Perhaps she picked on me because she thought "humorous" provocation might help me develop a less serious demeanor (My Aunt Lovella back in Cricket said I was the most serious child she had ever encountered), or maybe she simply liked me and was trying to communicate with an 8-year-old in the only way she knew how. Whatever her real motivation, she brought me close to tears a number of times with her "playful" badgering.

My favorite activity in the summertime at Mrs. Persinger's was taking command of the small pile of planks down in the backyard and in my active imagination, transforming the pile into a school classroom. I could fairly easily recruit some neighborhood kids as my pretend students. Always assuming the role of teacher, I authoritatively perched in the center of the woodpile, called roll, taught dubious history lessons, and tried to impose homework as well as discipline on my erstwhile students. (Interesting how that woodpile experience led to a Ph.D. and teaching at the college level.)

After we had lived in Roanoke about a year, Dad purchased the house adjacent to, but across a street from, Mrs. Persinger's. Similar to our former landlady's, our new residence was two-storied, but brick whereas Mrs. Persinger's was white frame. Although I still had to share a room with my sister, we reveled in what we considered lots of space. In all there were three bedrooms upstairs: Pat's and my bedroom, our parents' bedroom (where baby Angela slept), and a guest bedroom. Pat and I were happy that our room overlooked the street; we could keep an eye out for other kids' activities in the neighborhood. Sometimes when Dad's around-the-clock work schedule brought him home in the middle of the day, he would sleep in the spare bedroom. At the back of the house and painted a forest green, it afforded him more peace and quiet. He needed his sleep; he could be called back to drive his 16-wheeler any time after just four hours at home.

We had a half bath on the first floor, but the full bath on the second floor was the only one with a bathtub (sans shower). The upstairs bath saw a lot of action since that's where we all bathed.

In 1951 when we first moved into our new residence we still listened to the radio for entertainment at night. One of the programs we regularly tuned in to was Amos 'n Andy. Much to our present-day remorse, it never occurred to us then, having been raised in the South and with consciousness raising at least a decade away, that the show was totally racist. The two white guys (Freeman Godsen and Charles J. Correll) playing the respective roles of Amos and Andy generated great laughter, certainly among white America, with their inaccurate, stereotyped, prejudiced interpretation of black culture.[3]

Besides listening to the radio, another activity we enjoyed in our kitchen was gathering around the table and playing board games. Once in a while our Dad, friends, and another neighborhood father would join us in playing a lively and rather fiercely competitive game of Monopoly or Boom or Bust (another "capitalist" theme board game). Sometimes when school was not in session we played these games for hours on end.

In 1952, our parents finally purchased a family television set which they placed in the living room. We kids didn't spend much time watching it, though. In the first place, the small images on the 12" screen required a great deal of concentration. In the second place, it was a black and white t.v., not exactly riveting. Lastly, our choices were limited to only three channel broadcasts: NBC, CBS, and ABC. One program we did always try to catch, however, on Saturday night was *Your Hit Parade*. Sponsored by Lucky Strike Cigarettes, this show featured Snooky Lansen, Giselle McKenzie and others singing the top ten billboard hits of the week. Each song, such as "This Old

House" (actually made popular by Rosemary Clooney), "You Belong to Me," and "Teach Me Tonight," was featured on the program in a mini tableau, arguably a forerunner of modern day videos on MTV (Music Television) and CMT (Country Music Television).

When Dad wasn't working on the weekend (that was seldom), he liked to watch Friday Night Fights on the *Gillette Cavalcade of Sports*. One of the most memorable of those fights took place in 1951 between Joe Louis and Rocky Marciano. Audiences all over the U.S. watched as Louis, the Brown Bomber, heavyweight champion of the world and one of the most talented boxers in history, met his downfall at the mighty fists of the younger Marciano.[4]

Some of the earliest popular t.v. programs the rest of us Millers watched were: *The Goldbergs*, centered around a Jewish matriarch in the Bronx; *Mama*, a series based on the "Protestant-Norwegian Hansens of San Francisco"; *The Life of Riley*, portraying the escapades of a bumbling, inept main character, a father of Irish descent; Milton Berle's variety show, *Texaco Star Theater*; *What's My Line?*, a quiz show hosted by Garry Moore; *I Led Three Lives*, about a counterspy for the FBI; Ted Mack's *The Original Amateur Hour*; and for serious drama, shows such as *Fireside Theater*, *Playhouse 90*, or *The U.S. Steel Hour*. We, of course, followed *I Love Lucy*, the highest rated t.v. show from 1952-1955. Last but not least, debuting on television in 1953, the flamboyant, romantic pianist Liberace never failed to mesmerize us with his show.[5]

We didn't congregate in the living room only to watch t.v.; we often lounged there on our well-worn, dark blue upholstered furniture, entertained company, and Mama hosted our birthday parties there too. Although our house included a formal dining room, separated from the living room by French doors, most of the time we ate our meals in the kitchen. The half bath extended off the kitchen. Access to the backyard led from the kitchen through a narrow, latticed enclosed back porch, and down some stairs. The above described features of our house were common to many of the other homes in our neighborhood.

Two of my favorite places in the house included the basement and the front porch because it had a big, wooden-slatted swing attached to the ceiling. I spent many hours on the swing, sometimes daydreaming alone, and sometimes sitting and lolly-gagging with my friends. But our basement, divided into four dark, dusty rooms, particularly intrigued me. Residue from the former coal furnace still coated the walls, ceilings, and floors.[6] (By the time we bought it, our home was heated by oil.) The basement appealed to me in a Gothic romantic way–the gloom, the womb-like feel projected by the low ceilings, the neglected rooms offering dusky nooks and crannies to explore.

In my quest for yet another playhouse, I took on the project of trying to rid the basement of its coal remnants; with much sweeping and dusting, I succeeded to some extent.

Most importantly, I was thrilled to discover in one of these basement rooms a mannequin, a life-size store dummy, left by the former owners. For a child such as I who loved to pretend and could entertain myself indefinitely, having a dummy companion to play with was manna from heaven. Ay Dios, my good fortune was short-lived. Clarisse, the stringy haired, skinny little daughter of the former tenants, all too soon demanded the return of her mannequin. I did, however, still appropriate space in the basement where I whiled away many hours in make-believe.

Good fortune deserted me again a short while after the mannequin incident when, as I was bathing one night, I noticed a growth protruding immediately above and to the side of my right knee. I assumed I had somehow bumped my leg; I expected the hard knot to go away. When after many weeks the knot remained, I knew something was seriously wrong. Just what, I didn't know, but in my juvenile ignorance and trepidation I decided to hide my condition from my family. I took great pains to bathe and dress in total privacy so that my knee and the knot that had now grown to the size of a lemon never showed. Clandestine as I was, my older sister spotted the knot and threatened to tell Mama. Ultimately for my own good, Pat, in revenge for some dispute in which I had gained the upper hand, finally revealed my secret to Mama. She rushed me to the doctor whereupon he diagnosed a bone tumor and scheduled surgery at the upcoming close of school. The year was 1952, at the end of my fifth grade.

Between the time of the diagnosis and the scheduled surgery my parents and I feared the worst. For instance, one of my school chums told me that Mama had told her mother that the reason my parents had started me on violin lessons was because they wanted me to be involved in an activity which didn't require walking in the event that I lost my leg. As usual in a fearful situation, I reacted with dread and deep anxiety.

My feelings were not in the least assuaged when one of our well-meaning next door neighbors suggested that Mama take me to a faith healer by the name of Oral Roberts, scheduled soon in Roanoke to "lay hands" on the sick and the lame. Mr. Roberts, a relative newcomer in the business, had begun his ministry career in 1947 with the Pentecostal Holiness Church. The neighbor added that we would, of course, have to pay a fee for any miracle cure achieved by Mr. Roberts. Actually Roberts didn't charge an outright fee for his miracles or for the 2 ½ x 5" white cloths which he prayed over and then dispensed to believers. He just made sure recipients of any of his blessings put their names on a list which his organization later contacted for regular donations. Since my parents did not shepherd me to his tent revival (one of his tents could hold up to 12,500 souls), we missed out on the opportunity to meet the man who became a famous televangelist and who in 1965 founded Oral Roberts University in Tulsa, Oklahoma, famed for its basketball team.[7]

Mama and Daddy didn't subscribe to faith healing; for my malady they opted to continue affiliation with a licensed orthopedic surgeon. As the operation turned out, I didn't lose my leg but other complications arose. During the surgery the doctor found not only a large bone tumor but numerous smaller ones which had spread into my knee joint. These smaller tumors had not shown up in pre-operative X-rays. Anyway, the surgeon left the smaller tumors in place for the time being, to be removed only when I had attained my full adult height. He explained to us that growth in the leg originates in the joint and if that joint is hacked prematurely, growth is retarded. In other words, if he had removed all the tumors, I would have ended up a cripple with one leg shorter than the other. I had to wait until I was 17 before the second procedure was performed. Consequently, I spent the rest of my childhood subconsciously or consciously worried about the outcome of that surgery.

When I came home from the initial surgery Mama and Daddy had transformed our dining room into a makeshift recovery room. There I lay in bed, whiney, and pampered by everyone except my older sister, who refused to cater to a spoiled invalid. I sported a full-leg cast and walked for weeks on crutches. To my horror, when my cast and the stitches were finally removed, not only had my leg shrunk in circumference, the wound had not fully healed. The skin on both sides of the approximately seven-inch-long incision gaped open and ultimately formed a great deal of scar tissue. No one in our little sequestered universe even imagined plastic surgery to eradicate the ugly scars. Even if plastic surgery had been an option, we couldn't have afforded it.

Until I had the second surgery years later and the doctor cut away most of the original unsightly scar (the second scar was much less visible and ugly), I always tried to hide my unattractive leg. I felt so insecure about my skinny legs and disfigured right knee, I refused to wear shorts. In the seventh grade I even hid out in the girls' locker room during my indoor gym class one day rather than walk across the gymnasium in my short, one-piece gym suit in front of the boys' class. I should've confided in my mama about the extent of my self-consciousness but I never did. As in many families of that era, Mama expected us kids to fend for ourselves. Besides, she was busy with her chores or engrossed in her sometimes lengthy telephone conversations. I seldom interrupted her. Just like my grandparents, my mother and father also believed that children should not speak unless spoken to and should be seen but not heard. We kids kept low profiles.

Mama certainly wasn't absent from home. She nor any of the other mothers who lived near us worked outside the home; they fulfilled roles of housewife and mother. In our middle-class neighborhood, moms didn't usually participate in upper-class charitable organizations or civic groups such as arts councils and the like. As home duties permitted, however, Mama and most of the women in our neighborhood did volunteer work at church and school. Mama also belonged to and held office in The Fifth Wheel, the women's auxiliary club for the truck drivers of Associated Transport. The Wheel organized family picnics and dances for trucker couples and helped employees in times of illness or other family crises.

Mama possessed a talent for interacting well with others. Always empathetic and quite extroverted, she talked incessantly. I grew up a quiet child mainly because it was difficult for me to get in a word edgewise as we used to say. Visions of Mama sitting beside the telephone table, smoking a cigarette, and talking to her friends on the phone stay with me. She never met a stranger, a personality trait that sometimes embarrassed me as a child. I was mortified when she conversed non-stop with the furnace repair man, for instance. Her revelation to complete strangers of intimate details of our personal lives struck me, even at a tender age, as inappropriate. Nevertheless, I loved Mama intensely.

Mama loved all of her daughters and devoted herself to doing special things for each of us. For example, she always celebrated each of our birthdays. Sometimes she threw (what was considered then) elaborate birthday parties for one or the other of us. At one of my birthday parties, she invited my entire school class (and almost all came). Circled by my little school buddies all dressed in their party best, I tore into my pile of birthday presents with great glee. Mama served one of her famous homemade cakes along with lots of ice cream and organized games for us such as pin the tail on the donkey.

When Mama enlisted as room mother at school, she brought candy, homemade cupcakes and Kool Aid, all in flavors and colors suitable to the holiday or season. Mama's greatest contribution to the school activities of my siblings and me, however, lay in the spectacular costumes she designed and constructed for us to wear in school plays. For my lead role in our sixth grade Christmas play, Mama made me an awesome elf costume. She topped off the sturdy, realistic-looking, red and green felt costume with a pointy elf's hat and pointy little elf's boots. Decked out in my elf finery, I and a few of my classmates performed the play in our school assembly as well as for a local radio station. (I obviously outgrew my first grade stage fright.)

Not only did Mama make costumes, but she also sewed most of our dresses for school and church. Untold hours at the Singer sewing machine produced fetching homemade garments from colorful and attractive fabrics, cut out with the help of Simplicity and McCall dress patterns. We were happy enough to wear these unique clothes. Although I was ignorant of brand names, I did vaguely notice other children's clothes having a more sophisticated, manufactured look and being of heavier quality cloth, such as wool. Reflecting their mothers' department store shopping, my female peers wore more separates—blouses, sweaters, and skirts—than I did too. In the late '40s and early '50s almost none of my young friends or I wore slacks or jeans, but we did wear shorts in hot weather. For the cold winters in Roanoke my parents outfitted my siblings and me in store-bought woolen coats, scarves, and gloves.

Besides sewing, Mama laundered all our clothes while we children lived at home. Mama saw to all the housecleaning as well; we didn't begin cleaning our own rooms until we were teenagers. If that were not enough, Mama ceaselessly cooked, an expectation of lower and most middle class housewives. We Millers took our meals at home, seven days a week. Mama grocery shopped while we were in school. We left the house each morning fortified with a nourishing breakfast of fried eggs with either toast or sausage gravy and biscuits or hot cereal (oatmeal or cream of wheat). Once in a while we ate cold cereal. For one of our favorite combinations at breakfast, we mixed a small amount of Karo Syrup with a softened pat of margarine until it appeared an even caramel color. Then we sopped the concoction up with a biscuit and washed it down with a glass of milk. (The biscuits came out of a can; Mama quit making homemade biscuits when in the 1950s the canned variety hit the grocery store refrigerated section). The Karo Syrup/margarine/biscuit combination originated generations before from Appalachian ingenuity when there was nothing else in a poor household to eat. We never thought of the dish as poverty inspired, however; we simply relished the taste of it. It was comfort food.

For dinner, which we referred to as supper (we never used the term "dinner" for a meal at our house, only "lunch" and "supper"), we always shared a sit-down, ample, well-balanced meal together. Typical of southern tradition, we ingested a lot of fried meat, especially chicken or pork chops, served with gravy and fried apples, along with vegetable side dishes. Also common for Southerners, our family usually feasted on fried chicken on Sundays.[8] Sometimes we ate only a vegetarian plate consisting of pinto beans, onions, cucumbers, cornbread, and an additional vegetable, say fried squash. Mama always served sweet tea, a southern staple and our beverage of choice, with lunch and dinner. For dessert we gobbled up Mama's outstanding homemade berry cobblers or her banana or rice puddings.

Not only a good cook, Mama was innovative, always looking for new grocery store offerings and willing to experiment with new foods. In terms of meal preparation, store-bought canned goods in mid-20th century provided considerable options, not to mention relief, to housewives. Historically speaking, having such choice was a relatively new development. While the art of preserving fruit and wine by heating it in jars dates back at least as far as the Romans, it was not until the early 19th century that a wide array of food was proven suitable for canning. That's when a Frenchman by the name of Nicolas Appert through dogged experimentation figured out how to preserve comestibles, consistently safe to eat and tasty, in cannisters and bottles. In the United States it took the Civil War and the problem of feeding troops in the 1860s to acclimate a wide citizenry to eating from a can. Besides, until about mid-19th century, opening a tin of food usually required tools along the line of hammer and chisel, a manner of accessing victuals that could draw blood. Thankfully by the mid-20th century, refinement of both the can opener and the tin can dramatically reduced the hazards of reaching the contents. As people increasingly moved from rural to urban areas, grocery shelves in cities and towns brimmed with factory-produced canned goods, and millions of housewives like my mom readily served them up at meal time.[9]

Regardless of the widespread availability of canned goods, neither quality canned foods nor frozen ones were nearly as diverse or as plentiful in the 1950's as they became in the next half century. Preservation of food by freezing is another technique that's been around since ancient times but not commercially applied successfully and extensively until after Clarence Birdseye perfected the process in 1928. Still the U.S. populace remained generally skeptical about the safety and flavor of frozen foods until almost mid-20th century.[10] People become acculturated to certain types of foods prepared in particular ways; for any given populace to change their eating habits usually takes quite a while.

One uncommon culinary specialty in the early 50's in southwestern Virginia was pizza. Up to that point not many Roanokers routinely included pizza in their diets. Pizzerias and take-out pizza were new cultural additions to our area. My mother delightedly discovered homemade pizza when our next door neighbor's daughter, Marlene, during semester break from her home economics major in college, showed Mama how to make it. Mama promptly turned out her own delicious crust from scratch, topped with tomato sauce, abundant cheese, and sausage. As her experience with pizza making increased, she added a greater variety of toppings, such as pepperoni and green peppers. We kids devoured her tasty pizza, a nourishing meal in and of itself, with zeal. Not that we cared about nutrition. Mama's pizza complemented with a Coca-Cola "made our eyes light up and our stomachs say howdy," as the old southern song declares.

As much as we would've preferred pizza, sandwiches usually comprised our lunch fare. Mama packed sandwiches for us for lunch when we attended public school in Roanoke. During the summer months at home we were usually left to our own devices when lunch time rolled around. Our favorites combined baloney and tomato, or running a close second, we liked just sliced, homegrown tomatoes on white bread with mayonnaise. If Mama's grocery shopping was long overdue and the proverbial cupboard was bare, I could always depend on there being at least lettuce in the fridge, loaf bread, and mayonnaise and would throw together a sandwich of those three ingredients. We were also fond of peanut butter with sliced bananas sandwiches or even plain peanut butter ones or ones containing only sliced bananas; we garnished all these sandwiches with mayonnaise.

For an afternoon snack my pint-sized neighborhood friend, Kay, would on occasion offer me a raw wiener which she pulled directly out of her underpants. I usually declined her generosity although Kay's gesture was actually not as gross as it sounds. Rest assured, Kay bathed every day and put on a clean pair of underpants. Until she and I and the rest of the little girls in our neighborhood reached the age of about 10, we frequently wore, whether indoors or out, only white cotton briefs in the summertime. We dressed for the weather; Roanoke is humid in the summer, and our homes weren't air conditioned. Besides, our families had limited wardrobe funds, and our mothers had plenty to do besides the wearisome chore of washing clothes. So in her cotton briefs, not equipped with pockets, Kay utilized her only resource for storing things: the hot dog snack simply comprised part of her panty cargo.

Kay and I palled around a lot, having fun along with the rest of the neighborhood children. In the 1950s our Wasena neighborhood was a great place to grow up. Some adventure or activity always awaited us, all within walking distance and always safe. In the summertime, for instance, my older sister and I could walk without fear six blocks from our house in the evenings to Wasena Park and watch city league baseball games. We were never truly alone; not only our Mama but other neighborhood parents or their children knew where we were and what we were doing. If they thought it necessary, parents would reprimand others' children. Mothers, because so many of them did not work outside the home, created their own informal but quite effective neighborhood watch. In this close-knit community, we knew everybody for blocks around. Neighbors interacted on a daily basis. Weather permitting, we enjoyed being outside at our homes and walking wherever we needed to go. Front porches and front porch swings facilitated openness and togetherness, no doubt nosiness too, but no one seemed inordinately bothered by that.

Commuting neither existed as part of our reality nor our vocabulary. Downtown was only about three miles from where we lived. Most of our fathers' jobs were located in or around central city. In the urban center our mothers shopped at department stores for household items and clothing. For other shopping needs such as gasoline, groceries, medicine, and bakery goods, we walked merely two blocks: one block down Howbert, then left on Main Street, and in one more block began our small community stores.

The first building in our little shopping hub housed a modest-sized drugstore. At the soda fountain in the drugstore it was great fun for us kids to buy 5th Avenue or Mounds candy bars, or if in the rare case we had enough money, a milkshake or a toasted pimento cheese sandwich. Sometimes Mama would take us girls to the soda fountain and treat us to an inexpensive lunch. There were stools at the counter and tables and chairs if we wanted to sit down and eat on the premises. Located next door to the drugstore was a cramped, dimly lit, mom-and-pop grocery store which Mama utilized fairly frequently, especially when she ran out of a food item and didn't have time to go to a bigger grocery store.

It was fairly easy to fill the bill in grocery needs for middle-class home cooked meals in the 1950s. Expectations as well as selection of groceries in small towns were limited; the average palate had not been initiated into gourmet culinary tastes. Given the state of international trade and of our national transportation system at the time, Roanoke generally lacked access to the exotic agricultural produce from around the world. It was only in the mid-20th century in the United States that it became commercially worthwhile to outfit tractor-trailer rigs with refrigeration; the interstate highway system which makes it feasible for trucks to transport fresh produce from coast to coast wasn't even proposed until 1954 (under President Eisenhower). Consequently, we ate fresh produce basically from our locale when it was in season.

By happy chance for our Wasena neighborhood, though, we enjoyed quick access to an impressive array of desserts. Parcell's Pastries, on the other side of the mom-and-pop grocery store, specialized in confections such as chocolate eclairs and cream pies. As they made deliveries all over our side of town, their trucks were easily recognizable with the folksy slogan written on the back: "Don't bump me, I'm full of Parcell's Pastries."

Across the street from the drugstore, grocery store, and pie shop stood the service station. Unlike the majority of gas stations today, it truly provided a full range of services; the attendants pumped gas, washed windshields, checked under the hood, changed oil, performed mechanical work if needed, and checked the air in tires. The other service-oriented businesses located close by the gas station on Main Street included a beauty salon and a small furniture restoration shop.

Ours was a vibrant, youthful community. The bounty of young people, not just the children but their parents too, on Howbert Avenue reflected nationwide demographic patterns. Overwhelmingly, servicemen returning from WWII were of marriageable age. Most ex-servicemen either were married before they left for overseas or married soon after they returned to the States. Moreover, these men and their wives wanted children. People in the U.S. in the 1940s and '50s viewed having children as virtuous, economically viable, and even patriotic. Families added to the prosperity and growth of the nation. Many men in Wasena were veterans of WWII, one or two even veterans of the Korean War; the majority of them blessed with children. Thus on Howbert Avenue we had lots of playmates, varying in ages, interests, and personalities.

Although a couple of years younger than I, one of my constant neighborhood companions was Laura Ann. Laura, an only child, was beautiful, with naturally curly, short brown hair, a perfectly sculpted face, and olive skin. She and I would climb and play around the cherry tree in her backyard, wallow around half naked in the water runoff down the sides of Howbert Avenue after a heavy summer downpour, and play house on her front porch. To construct our playhouse, we simply turned the heavy, wooden porch chairs upside down and draped old bed sheets over top of them.

Laura Ann's mother frequently invited me to stay for lunch at their house, so often that I memorized a little poem her mom had framed on the wall:

> I wish I was a little rock
> a sittin' on a hill,
> nothin' doin' all day long
> but just a sittin' still.
> I wouldn't eat,
> I wouldn't sleep,
> I wouldn't even wash.
> I'd just sit there a million years
> and rest myself, by gosh.

> —Author Unknown

The poem typified Laura's sweet mother's lackadaisical personality, a demeanor which could be attributed to Mrs. Long's physical condition. Laura's mother suffered from a thyroid condition which manifested itself in a very conspicuous goiter around her neck. This affliction lingered in mid-20th century because of an earlier lack of iodine in people's diets. Some, but not all, with a goiter endure quite uncomfortable symptoms, e.g., a choking sensation when eating or labored breathing during sleep. In either case, the only way to get rid of a large goiter is to remove it surgically. Mrs. Long managed to get along without undergoing an operation.

Mr. Long, a journalist with the *Roanoke Times* newspaper, did not enjoy the best of health either. Laura, the apple of her father's eye, sadly lost him to a heart attack when she was still elementary school age. Even more tragic, Laura witnessed the fatal attack in her own living room. I think to make up for the trauma and the loss, her mother spoiled Laura Ann even more after Mr. Long died.

Laura for sure never stopped her mischievous behavior. For instance, one afternoon when I had gone over to her house to play, she chased me around for the pure fun of it with a butcher knife. I think I must have told her long before that I was afraid of knives ever since Paul in Cricket had "playfully" stabbed my older sister. She thought it a hoot to see me running scared.

Another friend of mine in the neighborhood was Penelope, sibling of my love interest, Donny (three years older than I, Donny was actually my sister's boyfriend, but I harbored a huge crush on him too). Although quite physically active, Penelope appeared fragile with her translucent fair skin, naturally platinum blonde hair, and slender build. I envied Penelope's tap and ballet lessons and would try to imitate the slap-ball-change dance step she showed me. When we could get our hands on some chalk, she and I played a mean game of hopscotch on Howbert Avenue sidewalks. On those same walks she and I also rollerskated, with the metal kind of skates that fitted under and onto the soles of our shoes. They had to be tightened with a key, which we each wore on a string around our neck. We took some spills and contended with quite a few bruised body parts when we skated because the many cracks and humps in our old, in-need-of-repair public sidewalks tripped us up sometimes.

Another of my pals, Jenny, who lived across the street from us and was the daughter of a nurse and an alcoholic lawyer father, frequently played dolls with me. We were crazy about our dolls; the more they resembled real babies, the more we adored them. My favorite doll happened to be male, similar in size to a six-month-old human baby. I knew its gender from its short, painted-on hair and facial features, of course; no doll baby of that era sported even a hint of genitalia. Jenny and I spent innumerable afternoons in the summer pretending we were mothers and our dolls were our babies. We fed our baby dolls from their play bottles, changed their diapers, dressed, undressed, cuddled and scolded them.

It was thanks to a brochure that Jenny's nurse mother gave us one summer that Jenny and I (I was 10 years old) learned where real babies came from. When her mother gave her the brochure, Jenny came racing across the street to share her risque literature with me. We took it into my backyard, sat under a dogwood tree in the shade, and voraciously read every word. The facts filled me with such wonderment that I anxiously sought out Mama's verification of it all after Jenny and I finished reading. She, I think, was only too happy to substantiate the biology lesson rather than explain it in full, graphic detail as the brochure had done. Mama and certainly Daddy never initiated a discussion of sex with us kids. If I ventured to ask Mama about sex, she would answer but not always in stellar fashion. Sex education was not part of the curriculum in public schools either. This state of ignorance yielded some preposterous and humorous (in retrospect) rumors among my peers, such as the myth that boys also wore sanitary pads once a month. I was never sure what for.

Dad not only assiduously avoided any human reproduction lessons for his offspring, but he also actually interacted very little with us under any circumstances. Driving a sleeper truck for Associated Transport kept him on the road most of the time. Dad and his partner would alternate between driving and sleeping in the truck, negating the need to stop some place to sleep. Except for meal breaks, the truck kept rolling. Sometimes we kids would go for weeks without seeing Dad because more times than not, when he finished a run he would return home in the middle of the night only to be called back to work four hours later. Dad persisted in this killer schedule because it earned him an excellent union salary, easily comparable to middle management pay in a white collar setting. In many ways he took pleasure in life on the road. Once in a while he would regale us with a story about what he saw or experienced, say in New York, New Jersey, or Pennsylvania, his most traveled territory.

So accustomed to his absence from home, we kids in a sense resented his return. For all intents and purposes we lived our daily lives in a single-parent household. Mama ruled our world but with a soft touch. When Dad was home, we either had to tiptoe around because he had to sleep, or, if he was awake, we had to follow his dictates. We kids hardly knew this man whose only role, or so it seemed to us, was to bully. A little in Dad's defense, Mama unquestionably took advantage of his stern disciplinarian role. She especially liked to defer to him when she believed we deserved serious physical punishment. She preferred he as the designated bad guy carry it out.

If we wanted money from Dad, we had to beg; he was extremely tight. Mother was equally penurious. Movie money, for example, was difficult to obtain. If we were gutsy enough to ask for it, we could expect the canned lecture on 1) how hard it was for Dad to earn money, 2) how we were acting so frivolously when the family needed money for other, infinitely more critical things, 3) how Mama needed surgery for one ailment or another and the family needed every penny to pay her medical bills. Despite all this, Dad somehow managed to buy a new car every other year. He claimed he bought it for the family. We couldn't wait to grow up and earn our own money.

During Dad's waking hours at home his fatalistic world view and rigid moral standards (Grandmother Miller profoundly influenced him) cast a gloomy pall on our plans and activities, no matter how simple or innocent they were. He intimidated, criticized, accused, and vetoed. Of course, it was not uncommon in the 1950s for fathers to be strict, and breadwinning men were expected to play the dominant role in the family. But if the breadwinners' work didn't demand long absences, hopefully the children of such men were exposed to other facets of their father's personality besides ogre and party pooper, to borrow a term from the 1950s comedian, George Gobel. In Dad's case, we had little chance of knowing the whole person who was our father.

In hindsight I fully appreciate that my father, and hoards of other men of his generation and background, took and remained at whatever jobs, however arduous, they could obtain in order to provide for their families. For one thing, Dad and his cohorts were just old enough to have witnessed the heart-breaking effects of mass unemployment during the Great Depression. I suspect, too, for those men who had survived WWII service, their tolerance level for drudge work may have been relatively higher than average. Probably on some level, ex-servicemen were simply thankful to be alive, to be back in the U.S.A., and to be able to earn a living.

NOTES

1. Our family moving to Roanoke from North Wilkesboro is a perfect example of two phenomena: chain migration and the high mobility of American families. Chain migration occurs when individuals have moved to a new geographic location, found it more desirable (usually economically) than their former locale, whereupon their relatives, and sometimes their friends, later join them. With or without chain migration entailed in moving, Americans are highly mobile. Mobility increased fairly rapidly after WWII, with wider ownership of automobiles, the job demands of stepped up industrialization and urbanization, mounting suburbanization, and a greater emphasis on the independent nuclear family.

2. The Teamsters Union has suffered from notoriety by association with mob bosses, especially from around the mid-20th century. Nevertheless, many members, including my father, remain loyal to the organization because they have derived decent salaries, and ample health and retirement benefits through the Teamsters. Now known as the IBT, or International Brotherhood of Teamsters, it was founded in 1903 as a craft union for drivers of a team of oxen or a wagon drawn by a horse or mule. The IBT logo depicting two horse heads facing away from each other, with a wheel with spokes under them, still reflects its origins.

3. Doherty, 70.

4. Margolick, 2005.

5. Doherty, see Chs. 3 & 7.

6. Before the switch over to oil, coal provided the greatest energy source in the United States, including heat for private homes. In southwestern Virginia, coal was a relatively affordable commodity because of the abundance of coal in that region of the country. The Norfolk and Western Railway (now the Norfolk and Southern) readily transported coal throughout the area and beyond.

7. Oral Roberts' career later took a number of downturns. For instance, in 1977 he raised enough money to open a medical school complex at his university, only to have

it fail by the 1990s. In addition, Roberts through the years lost credibility when he reported a) having talked to Jesus and seen that he was 900 feet tall, and b) God having spoken to him and informed him that if he didn't raise $5 million for his ministry that God was going to call him home. Harrell, 1985.

8. ". . . [I]n the 1950's, meals were straightforward, governed by the days of the week rather than a sense of culinary adventure: meatloaf with ketchup Mondays, macaroni and cheese casserole Tuesdays, beef stew on Thursdays." Nathan, 71.

9. Shephard, 228, 245-46, 253.

10. Shephard, 305-308.

SUGGESTED READINGS

Barfield, Ray. *Listening to Radio*. Westport, Conn.: Praeger, 1996.

Doherty, Thomas. *Cold War, Cool Medium: Television, McCarthyism, and American Culture*. New York: Columbia UP, 2003.

Harrell, David Edwin, Jr. *Oral Roberts: An American Life*. Bloomington, Ind.: Indiana UP, 1985.

Layman, Richard, ed. *American Decades: 1950-1959*. Detroit: Gale Research, 1994.

Margolick, David. *Beyond Glory: Joe Louise vs. Max Schmeling, and a World on the Brink*. New York: Knopf, 2005.

Marling, Karal Ann. *As Seen on TV: The Visual Culture of Everyday Life in the 1950s*. Cambridge, Mass.: Harvard UP, 1994.

Morris, T. N. "Management and Preservation of Food." Pp. 26-52 in *A History of Technology*, edited by C. Singer et al. Vol. 5. Oxford: Clarendon, 1958.

Nathan, Joan. "Red, White, and Blueberry," *U.S. News & World Report*. (15/22 Aug. 2005): 71.

Shephard, Sue. *Pickled, Potted and Canned*. New York: Simon & Schuster, 2000.

Thorne, Stuart. *The History of Food Preservation*. Kirby Lonsdale, Cumbria, England: Parthenon, 1986.

Witwer, David Scott. *Corruption and Reform in the Teamsters Union*. Urbana, Ill.: University of Illinois Press, 2003.

Chapter Five

Lessons Learned in School and Out: Social Class, Sexism, and the Bomb

In mid-school year 1950 we moved from tiny Cricket to Roanoke, population 91,921 at the time, nestled in a narrow valley immediately west of the Blue Ridge Mountains of Virginia.[1] We quickly discovered that Roanoke is referred to as The Star City of the South after the massive man-made star erected there atop Mill Mountain in 1949. According to local history, the Roanoke Merchants Association conceived the notion of a star while trying to come up with a gimmick to jump start shopping for the Christmas season. It was the Chamber of Commerce, however, who apparently made the decision to keep the all-white star lit at night throughout the year. (Since then both red and blue neon stars have been added, framed within the larger white one.) The 88.5' high star sits on top of another unique feature of Roanoke, Mill Mountain itself, lying within the city limits, rising 800' above the town and not physically adjoined to any range of mountains. It is well nigh impossible to live within the city and not see the star, illuminated at night with 2,000 feet of florescent tubing, on top of the mountain.[2] For one of our first family outings in Roanoke, we drove the short but circuitous route up Mill Mountain and, standing in front of the base of the star, looked out upon our little metropolis and the surrounding Roanoke Valley, a scenic view whether at night or in the daytime. Looking down, we could almost distinguish, not far from the foot of Mill Mountain, our new neighborhood, Wasena.

I had much to surmount in these new environs, one of which was adjusting to the third grade at Wasena School. As a transfer, I found myself struggling to keep up in a more advanced educational system than that of my former Miller's Creek. To add to my initial discomfort in the new school, my classmates made fun of my western Carolina twang. Wasena at that time was also located in the wealthiest school district in town. Consequently, some of the students at Wasena hailed from distinctly affluent families, a social background quite unlike mine. With awe I witnessed a little friend of mine, and son of a medical doctor, being chauffeured every day to school in a Cadillac by his very chic, glamorous blonde mom. In contrast, our mom picked us up only once in a while, and likely as not, she showed up wearing an old house dress, sometimes with curlers in her hair. My older sister and I almost always walked the one or so miles to school and back; now and then we walked home for lunch. In those days we traipsed throughout our neighborhood with little fear of abduction or molestation.

Another big difference between my education in North Carolina and Virginia was the emphasis, certainly in Roanoke public schools, on state history. In third and fourth grades our teachers devoted large units of study to Virginia history. I quickly learned the fortuitousness of Old Dominion citizenship. As the plaque on my husband's distant relative's wall reads:

> To be a Virginian/either by birth, marriage, adoption/
> or even on one's mother's side/is an introduction to any state in the Union/
> a passport to any foreign country/
> and a benediction from the Almighty God.[3]

> —Author Unknown

After all, most all of the early presidents, not to mention a multitude of founding fathers, of the United States resided in Virginia, the largest of the thirteen original colonies. Moreover, many of these illustrious ancestors built grand, fascinating homes, such as Washington's Mt. Vernon and Jefferson's Monticello, which one can visit today. In fact, when I was a child, visiting Monticello constituted a standard seventh grade field trip for some Roanoke schools. Last but not least, descendants of numerous great statesmen of early America continue to reside in Virginia. Although some folks may recognize FFV merely as a cookie brand name, the FFVs or First Families of Virginia, such as the Randolphs, the Lees, the Monroes, and the Henrys, in the 1950s commanded a social status unattainable by more recent generations to the state. (Some progeny of renowned Virginian historical figures still work hard to preserve their exclusive social standing. Still others resort to all manner of social climbing to be admitted into that exclusive group.)

The Roanoke school system also required us to learn city history. We read in our texts that Roanoke was formerly known as Big Lick because of the naturally abundant salt licks that attracted large deer and other animals. Since animals congregated in the area, hunters followed. The earliest such hunters in our area were American Indians, among them the Cherokee and the Shawnee. Present-day place names in the city reflect the former Indian presence; the word "Roanoke" itself is supposedly derived from the Algonquin Indian name for shell money. Along the pedestrian route known as the Great Path, Big Lick in southwestern Virginia offered a central location where Amerindians could traverse the great Appalachian Mountain chain.[4]

In 1882, when a forerunner of the Norfolk and Western Railway (N & W) established its headquarters in Big Lick, the town changed its name to Roanoke, after the Roanoke River of Indian nomenclature. Roanoke became incorporated as a city in 1884, at which time the population numbered a little over 5,000. Such companies as Virginia Bridge and Iron were founded initially and continued to thrive because of Roanoke's natural resources and transportation advantages. Utilizing water from the Roanoke River, the city from early on provided power to support such enterprises as an innovative electric street car system. Manufacturers also drew on the locally abundant materials of lumber and lime for building and for turning out cement and plaster. Roanoke's growth was so remarkable that locals dubbed it the Magic City. Regardless of its many other successes, Roanoke essentially grew up around and flourished with the advancement of the railroad, whose multiple tracks still dominate the downtown landscape.[5]

Especially in the latter nineteenth and early twentieth centuries railways played a crucial role in transporting coal, a major energy source for the rapidly industrializing United States. Not only southwestern Virginia, where Roanoke is located, but neighboring states, particularly West Virginia, supplied eastern regions of the U.S. with plentiful bituminous (hard) coal. In 1948 in the booming post-war economy, Norfolk and Western train cars hauled over 6,500,000 tons of coal to Roanoke and throughout the valley.[6] By the time my family had moved to the Star City of the South, the N & W was still heavily engaged in coal conveyance. Nineteen-fifty-one marked the peak year in the U.S. in quantity and quality for coal, soon to relinquish its dominance because of the beginning of the Oil Century.[7]

In Roanoke, the massive railroad shops, where the N & W cars and huge engines were (and still are) repaired, present a prominent feature along the railroad tracks. On the side of the railroad tracks opposite the city center stand other historic buildings associated with Norfolk and Western: two huge, adjacent buildings which housed the offices of N & W, and across the street, erected in the center of an elegantly landscaped ten acres, the rambling, beautiful, half-timber style Hotel Roanoke. At the turn of the century one could readily access the hotel from the N & W train station. From the earliest days of the railroad, vacationers and traveling business people alike enjoyed the regal decor, hospitality, and delicious southern cuisine offered by the hotel. On the menu of the gracious dining room, one can still order its famous peanut soup and spoon bread. Through the years, locals too have utilized the hotel for Sunday dinners, meetings, high school proms, and balls, not to mention for hosting dignitaries such as the state governor.

When I was a fifth grader, a photographer from the *Roanoke Times and World News* came to our elementary school looking for a supposed stereotypic student for an N & W newspaper advertisement. Low and behold, they selected me. I suppose my long, thick brown pigtails, tied with brightly colored grogram ribbon, attracted the photographer's attention. His photograph of me sitting behind a school desk, attired in one of the little dresses Mama had sewn for me, appeared in a whole page N & W ad in the newspapers of all the cities where the railroad ran. The territory spanned a multi-state area. When the ad came out in their local papers in North Carolina, Grandpa Church, Granddaddy and Grandmother Miller, all my aunts and uncles and cousins alike were abuzz with my new found fame.

Hardly any of my female peers wore pigtails, so mine served as a trademark and perhaps my crowning glory, that is, until the sixth grade when Mama cut my hair and permed it. She had grown tired of my fussing and squirming when she attempted to brush the tangles out of my nearly waist-length tresses. Plus, I agreed with her that I was getting a little too grown up for pigtails. Hair sheared to just below my ears took some getting used to by me as well as by some of my little boyfriends. One morning when I was standing in line waiting for school to commence, one of those boys clued me in that I was not so cute without braids. He called out, "Hey, Beautiful" right behind me. When I looked around at him, honestly more out of curiosity than vanity, he cruelly blurted out, "Not you, pie face." So much for fame and beauty.

Each morning when we arrived at Wasena Elementary we had to form lines according to our class and teacher. We remained in our orderly lines, parallel with the front of the school building, twelve lines in all, six on one side of the front door and six on the other, until the school day officially began. At the exact hour, our principal, Mrs. Roberts, emerged from the building and rang her hand-held school bell. After she clanged the bell, we marched one line after the other into our respective classrooms. We knew better than to challenge Mrs. Roberts' authority; with her red hair always perfectly coifed, her dress impeccable, and her no-nonsense demeanor, she ruled at school.

I was taken aback when one summer I learned that our very capable and somewhat intimidating principal had suffered a nervous breakdown. As in my mother's case, I have no idea what specific malady Mrs. Roberts had to contend with; I seem to recall her telling Mama that her mental well-being depended upon daily regiment. Perhaps it was difficult for her to cope in the summertime without a rigid school term work agenda. In any case, when she returned to school in the fall, our little world again felt secure.

Not only did our principal at Wasena excel at her job, so did most of our teachers, all of whom were female. When I was a child, males rarely taught in elementary public schools, certainly not in our town. The two main reasons for the absence of males had to do with gender stereotyping and money. In mid-twentieth century it was generally believed that women were, by nature, better suited to work with children than were men. Second, the sexist logic of the day contended that men couldn't support their families on a teacher's salary (according to 1950s Census data, this ranged anywhere from $3,000 to $5,000, depending on location) while it was assumed that women weren't breadwinners and hence could live on a low salary. Interestingly, although school teaching paid very little, it attracted some of the finest female minds. For one thing, teaching was considered an honorable occupation. On the other hand, innumerable intelligent women may have chosen the field of education for lack of other options. Besides teacher, the careers of nurse, librarian, and secretary were deemed by families and the greater society to be the most appropriate for the so-called "weaker" sex.

Some of our most gifted teachers at Wasena specialized in music. In each elementary grade in Wasena the curriculum always included music as well as art. Our regular classroom teachers conducted our art lessons, but we had floating music teachers, i.e., teachers who came regularly to our school but taught each classroom only once or twice a week for an hour. Nonetheless, the music program at Wasena School and in Roanoke City Schools in general during the 1950s was high quality. Our regularly scheduled music instruction was one of the aspects of school I loved most.

One of the highlights of my elementary school days at Wasena was being invited by our music teacher, Mrs. Grayson, to appear on a t.v. community affairs program and to demonstrate how a simple tune could be played on water glasses. For the show a classmate, Billy, and I masterfully played "Twinkle, Twinkle Little Star" on our aquatic instruments. Our rendition proved a big hit with the audience at home, mainly consisting of our parents, other teachers, and schoolmates. I guess that incident qualified as Billy's and my 15 minutes of fame that Andy Warhol would later predict for the average person in modern society.[8]

Fancying myself having some singing talent, I appreciated any opportunity, at school or at home, to break into song. Besides gossiping and talking about boyfriends on our front porch swing, I sometimes entertained friends (or just myself) by singing. I would sing songs I had learned from Mama, for instance, the lullaby "My Little Buckaroo;" or from the radio, "You Belong to Me;" or from music class in elementary school, "Wagon Wheels."

School music was designed to help us enjoy and appreciate that particular art and sometimes to augment our other studies, such as history. The verses of "Wagon Wheels," e.g., paid tribute to the hardships of the early American pioneers who crossed the plains in Conestoga wagons:

> Westward we roll 'or the prairie,
> Riding from daybreak 'til night.
> No town in which we may tarry.
> No friendly cabins in sight.
>
> Wagon wheels, firm and strong
> Ride 'or desert and plain.
> All day long, roll along
> through the sunshine and rain.

—Author unknown

In contrast, one of our oft sung neighborhood ditties, whose only redeeming feature was to take some of the fear out of death by making light of it, went thus:

> Did you ever wonder when the hearse goes by
> if you might be the next to die?
> They wrap you up in a big, white sheet
> and bury you down about 6 feet deep.
> All goes well for about a week
> and then your coffin begins to leak.
> The worms crawl in, the worms crawl out.
> The worms play pinocle on your snout.
> Your stomach turns a slimy green
> and pus runs out like whipping cream.
> You sop it up with a piece of bread
> and that's what you eat when you're dead.

—Author unknown

As kids also find solace in pure silliness, we sang other gems, such as "Found a Peanut," which closely rivals "100 Bottles of Beer on the Wall" for redundancy, and "Weiner Man," which seems a bit suggestive but actually isn't lewd. It goes:

> I love my wiener man
> He owns a wiener stand
> He sells most anything from wieners on down
> Someday I'll marry him and be his wiener wed
> Hot dog! I love my wiener man.

—Author unknown

A naughty song that we did sing but really didn't comprehend the implications of went like this:

> I hear ya' knockin' but ya' can't come in
> I got on my nightie and it's mighty thin
> I need the money but I know it's a sin
> So quit your knockin' and come on in.

—Author unknown

Fortunately we learned more respectable lyrics from our music teachers. Not only did we learn songs at school, but we also all were taught how to play simplistic melodies on a metal flute. One beak-nosed, snobby, well-dressed, middle-aged flute teacher of ours in the fifth grade brooked no disobedience or inattention; she didn't hesitate to grab a disorderly or inattentive student's hand, turn it palm up, and while forcing the fingers of the hand back, whack the palm with her metal flute. Abusive? By today's standards, yes, but she not only grabbed a hand, she grabbed our attention.

While not particularly fond of our flute teacher, I cherished my fifth grade classroom teacher, Miss Johnson, freshly graduated from Longwood College in Farmville, Virginia. Teachers' colleges throughout the United States in the 1950s churned out thousands of women qualified for the profession. When I first came to Miss Johnson's classroom, with temerity and a completely naive perspective, I questioned her ability to teach. I mean I literally tried on occasion to suggest methods of my former teachers to her. Luckily for me Miss Johnson was a tolerant and patient woman. Soon I grew to idolize her because of both her mental and physical attributes. I came to admire her so much, in fact, that I accepted whatever she taught us as the everlasting, gospel truth. When she repeatedly admonished us to practice good health habits, such as eating fresh fruits and vegetables every day, she made a disciple out of me. Another one of her favorite pieces of advice, "Get at least eight hours of sleep every night; you can never really make up for lost sleep," impacts my quotidian routine to this day.

Quite lovely, blonde and lissome, Miss Johnson was also highly capable and innovative in her teaching techniques. One of the pedagogical cutting-edge projects she involved us in was a mock presidential election. In that year,1952, Dwight D. Eisenhower and Adelai Stevenson vied for the highest office in the land. Miss Johnson wanted us to learn first hand about how a person gets elected to the presidency. In our mock presidential race, my friend, Sammy, ran as Eisenhower on the Republican ticket for president and I ran as Stevenson on the Democratic ticket. Over several school days he and I had to present our respective party platforms to the class, after which they voted.

Sammy and I made a friendship pact that we would vote for each other. Sammy kept his end of the bargain, but I don't recall exercising similar integrity when I cast my vote.

Most of us in Miss Johnson's classroom were ignorant about both the machinations of our republican form of government and politics in general. We had no inkling of the insidious and overtly evil implications of McCarthyism, rampant at the time. I do remember, however, my parents being big fans of President Truman, at least before he fired General McArthur. The majority of my peers and I knew or cared little about current world affairs such as the Cold War, the Korean War, or revolutionary-torn China.

In 1946, when my cohorts and I were only four years old, Winston Churchill proclaimed, because of Joseph Stalin's totalitarian tactics and the impenetrability of the Soviet Union by outsiders, that an Iron Curtain had fallen across central Europe. The Communist Bloc Countries from behind the curtain operated both openly and clandestinely to undermine the democracies of the world through the spread of communism. Supposedly, the war between communism and democracy could ultimately be won or lost through the spread of ideologies, not necessarily through the armed forces of the Superpowers, the United States and the U.S.S.R. (The Union of Soviet Socialist Republics), actually facing each other on a blazing battlefield. After 1949, with the Russians' new-found atomic capability, in lieu of a U.S. versus U.S.S.R. conflagration, we learned to live in a world of mutual deterrence or a balance of terror. Hence the term "Cold War."

The Cold War between the United States and the Soviet Union manifested itself in proxy wars; i.e., countries backed by either the U.S. or the U.S.S.R. fought against each other on their native soil. Therefore, proxy wars occurred in various parts of the world, such as on the African continent, in central America, and in Asia. The Korean War (technically a United Nations police action that lasted from 1950 to 1953) was one such war, a hot war fought under the auspices of the cold one. Mao se Tung, the leader of the communist government of China, sent Chinese troops across the border to strengthen the North Korean Communist Army in its fight against an ostensibly democratic South Korea. The free world, including the United States, fought against the Communists to protect the sovereignty of South Korea.

The commander of American troops in Korean, the arrogantly aggressive McArthur, then pressured a more politically astute Truman to declare war on China. Truman could not condone McArthur's bellicose posturing and dismissed the general from his post. I remember the dramatic closing of McArthur's famous speech to Congress: "Old soldiers never die. They just — fade — away." His speech was met with thunderous applause.

For us young ones, the reality of the Cold War entailed more of a nagging fear than specific knowledge. We were subjected to visible and audible signs

of the Cold War, though. They consisted of the regularly broadcast, brief practice air raid alerts on television–"This is a test of the Emergency Broadcast-
ing System"—and the loud blaring throughout our city of the air raid signal
at noon every Saturday. In the 1950s Roanoke organized (apparently not too
successfully) Civil Defense units to try to spot any enemy aircraft in the skies,
to handle potential evacuations and to supply medical aid.[9]

During the 1950s motion pictures as well as television produced films and
programs confirming the dreadful, annihilative power of nuclear bombs. For
instance, in the spring of 1953 as a public service to the nation, the Atomic
Energy Commission (AEC) in conjunction with the Civil Defense Administration (CDA) sponsored a live television broadcast on CBS, NBC, and ABC
of an atomic explosion on Doom Town at Yucca Flat, culminating with the
ominous mushroom cloud and evanesced mannequins and fake homes.[10] The
Department of Defense together with the AEC also produced a classic film,
Operation Ivy, about the terrifying capabilities of a hydrogen bomb explosion. This 28-minute movie demonstrating the obliteration of a Pacific atoll
was shown on television multiple times in 1954 and was widely distributed to
public schools for classroom viewing.[11]

Our teachers periodically showed us such films, which incorporated in-
structions on how to survive a nuclear assault. The briefings encouraged our
families to build an underground bomb shelter in our respective backyards
and to keep it well-stocked with potable water and canned food. The school
movies didn't mention a safety measure which crossed many minds: keeping
a loaded shotgun handy in case shelterless neighbors tried to commandeer
one's refuge and supplies. If an actual air raid occurred while we were at
school, the movies demonstrated how we should jump under our desks and
cover our heads with our arms. Even to my young mind, these precautions
came across as illusory and ineffective against a nuclear attack. The horror of
a nuclear specter and the futility of warding off the aftermath haunted me.

It's no wonder that behavioral pundits dubbed the era in the U.S. after
WWII as The Age of Anxiety. The Red Scare promulgated especially by Wis-
consin Senator Joseph McCarthy and his cronies fueled U.S. citizens' para-
noia about communism. Even we children were familiar with the epithets
"better dead than red" and "dirty, pinko commie." True, some U.S. citizens
had empathized with the overthrow of governments which for centuries had
subjugated Chinese peasants and Russian serfs; some Americans even joined
the U.S. Communist Party. However, it may have been the case that many
erstwhile U.S. Communists endorsed egalitarianism more than revolutionary
bloodshed. Regardless, McCarthy, a master propagandist, thrived on the fame
and power commie-baiting afforded him. For starters, he trumped up evidence of a communist menace within our own government. In 1950 at a dinner speech for the Republican Women's Club in Wheeling, West Virginia,

McCarthy announced his infamous "list of 205 known communists in the State Department."[12] To enhance his own career, he gladly hyped the red peril.

Undercover agents claimed that Hollywood also teemed with reds. The House on Un-American Activities subpoenaed various members of the entertainment industry, including the popular, all-American icon Lucille Ball, to testify regarding alleged communist activities. In another case, in 1950 the FBI investigated the American hero Jonas Salk for a possible commie link based on his associations at the University of Michigan and his membership in the American Labor Party.[13] The witch hunts died out fairly soon, however, when in 1954 the chain-smoking Edward R. Murrow on his television program *See It Now*, exposed McCarthy and his antics.

Other factors besides McCarthyism contributed to the general fear in the U.S. during the 1950s.[14] President Eisenhower and his advisors subscribed to a foreign policy based on the domino theory: the belief that if one country fell to communism, then another, and then another would fall, as in the game of dominoes. This theory gained credence as two huge geo-political areas of the world, China and the USSR, successfully swallowed up more and more adjacent territories in the name of a new world order. At the very least, Americans sensed something out there lurking, threatening our way of life.

Youngsters such as I weren't immune to the foreboding atmosphere even if we didn't fully comprehend the causes of it. Miss Johnson alleviated some of our sense of doom by helping us understand, albeit at the most basic level, how the political process worked both at home and globally. Ironically, in today's slang, I could sing Miss Johnson's praises by referring to her as "da bomb" (this means the tops, the zenith, or the ultimate).

Miss Johnson also won my heart on another level: she let me do most all of the art work needed to decorate our classroom. Bulletin boards, large and small, hung in several places on the walls. While my classmates busied themselves with academic tasks, I stood at a table in the back of the room drawing on and cutting construction paper or painting watercolor scenes on poster-board-size sheets of plain white art paper. For fall decor I typically drew and painted children walking to school along a path strewn with brightly colored leaves. Christmas offered a potpourri of artistic themes for me, ranging from Santa Claus and elves to Christmas trees and fireplaces hung with stockings. I eagerly drew or painted them all. For spring I festooned bulletin boards with daffodils, robins feeding their young, and specifically for Easter, baskets, eggs, and bunnies. Art, along with music, greatly contributed to my enthusiasm for school.

Before school started in the fall of my sixth grade, I came in at Miss Johnson's request in preparation for her new class and again decorated her bulletin boards. My new sixth grade teacher, Miss Leighton, was not as avid a fan of my artwork as Miss Johnson. Nevertheless, the school system again granted me an outstanding educator in the person of Miss Leighton, and she did let me do some art work for her too. We students grumbled among ourselves that she was too strict, but on an unspoken level we recognized her excellent teaching abilities. She held us to the highest standards in our studies, yet she continually provided opportunities for fun learning activities. In addition, she gave us responsibility to carry out certain assignments by ourselves. For instance, she allowed us every morning, before we began our academic work, to plan and execute a short devotional program. Although we came up with a variety of observances, most of the time we read Bible verses no matter what else we included. Every now and then I sang a capella *The Lord's Prayer* for my part in daily devotions. After our brief religious ceremony we always stood up, hand over heart, and recited the Pledge of Allegiance to the Flag.

We considered Miss Leighton "old" (although she was probably only in her 50s) and were acutely aware that she was unmarried and wore a wig. What's more, we could tell she was totally bald beneath her wig. We, of course, snickered behind her back about her baldness and her wig. Still, we respected her. She lived in our Wasena neighborhood, only two streets over from my house. Once in the summer after I had completed my sixth grade year with her, a couple of my friends and I walked over and visited her at her home. Even as a twelve-year-old I noticed how immaculately she kept her house; it occurred to me even in my immaturity that she lived what she taught. For example, she lectured us to wash fresh fruit very thoroughly before eating it. Sure enough, that day at her house I noticed her obviously scrubbed apples in a sparkling glass bowl gracing the middle of her perfectly clean kitchen table.

Months after our visit to her house, it saddened me to learn that Miss Leighton had committed suicide. Having always viewed her as an eccentric, we were not altogether surprised by her drastic action. No adult ever conjectured, at least not around me, as to the cause of Miss Leighton's suicide. Her baldness a tell-tale clue of radiation treatment, she may have suffered unbearably from cancer, a disease usually tantamount to a death sentence in the 1950s. In any event, her death meant a definite loss to our community's educational system.

NOTES

1. Roanoke City has increased its population very little since 1950. According to the U.S. Census Bureau, in the year 2000, Roanoke residents numbered 94,911.

2. White, 1982.

3. In the last few years I've seen this same Virginia "loyalty" expression on a number of articles, including cocktail napkins and coffee mugs.

4. Jacobs, 92.

5. Jacobs, 119-121.

6. Lambie, 294.

7. Lambie, ix.

8. Andy Warhol was the famous pop artist, particularly known for his redundant portrayals on silk screen of contemporary objects such as Campbell Soup cans and of celebrities such as Marilyn Monroe.

9. White, 112.

10. Doherty, 10

11. Doherty, 12.

12. Doherty, 14.

13. Oshinsky, 147.

14. Eisenhower himself delivered an address on TV on April 5, 1954, entitled "Multiplicity of Fears." Doherty, 101.

SUGGESTED READINGS

Barson, Michael. *"Better Red Than Dead": A Nostalgic Look at the Golden Years of Russiaphobia, Red-Baiting, and Other Commie Madness*. New York: Hyperion, 1992.

Blair, Clay. *The Forgotten War: America in Korea, 1950-1953*. New York: Times Books, 1987.

Boyer, Paul. *By the Bomb's Early Light: American Thought and Culture at the Dawn of the Atomic Age*. New York: Pantheon, 1985.

Caute, David. *The Great Fear: The Anti-Communist Purge Under Truman and Eisenhower*. New York: Simon & Schuster, 1978.

Doherty, Thomas Patrick. *Cold War, Cool Medium: Television, McCarthyism, and American Culture*. New York: Columbia University Press, 2003.

Donovan, Robert J. *Conflict and crisis: The Presidency of Harry S. Truman, 1945-1948*. New York: Norton, 1972.

———. *Tumultuous Years: The Presidency of Harry S. Truman, 1949-1953*. New York: Norton, 1982.

Fried, Richard M. *Nightmare in Red: The McCarthy Era in Perspective*. New York: Oxford UP, 1990.

Hastings, Max. *The Korean War*. New York: Simon & Schuster, 1987.

Henriksen, Margot A. *Dr. Strangelove's America: Society and Culture in the Atomic Age*. Berkeley: University of California Press, 1997.

Hoover, J. Edgar. *Masters of Deceit: The Story of Communism in America and How to Fight It*. New York: Henry Holt, 1958.

Jacobs, E. B. *History of Roanoke City and History of the Norfolk and Western Railway Co*. Roanoke, Va.: Stone Printing Co., 1912.

Lambie, Joseph T. *From Mine to Market: The History of Coal Transportation on the Norfolk and Western Railway.* New York: New York UP, 1954.

Laurence, William L. *The Hell Bomb.* New York: Knopf, 1951.

Manchester, William Raymond. *American Caesar: Douglas MacArthur.* Boston: Little, Brown, 1978.

Moss, Norman. *Men Who Play God: The Story of the H-Bomb and How the World Came to Live With It.* New York: Harper and Rowe, 1968.

Oshinsky, David M. *Polio: An American Story.* Oxford, N.Y.: Oxford UP, 2005.

Ridgway, Matthew. *The Korean War.* New York: Doubleday & Co., 1967.

Smith, Robert. *MacArthur in Korea.* New York: Simon & Schuster, 1982.

Weart, Spencer R. *Nuclear Fear: A History of Images.* Cambridge, Mass.: Harvard UP, 1988.

White, Clare. *Roanoke 1740 - 1982.* Roanoke, Va.: Hickory Printing, 1982.

Chapter Six

Best Friends and the Loss of Naiveté

Regardless of my blue-collar, Appalachian background, by coincidence my closest friends in Wasena Elementary hailed from well-to-do families. My behavior used to grate on my mother's nerves when I returned to our humble abode after having visited in these affluent friends' homes. She contended that I acted malcontent, not to mention uppity, after I had luxuriated in the high standard of living at Annie Faye Johnson's and Sammy Reynold's, my greatest pals. Indeed, their homes did expose me to a different world.

I often spent the night at the Johnson home (Annie Faye slept over at my house too, once or twice, but we preferred her place because it held infinitely more rich adventures than mine), which stood on an eight to ten acre plot of land. One entered the property via a long, curving asphalt driveway leading up to the back entrance of the house. The house itself stood at the top of a hill, affording a splendid view of surrounding hills, other lovely homes in the community, and the Blue Ridge Mountains in the distance. On one side of the dwelling, extending further uphill, was a stand of forest, mostly pine trees. From the front of the house, the level yard gradually gave way to a long slope to a seldom traveled, neighborhood road at the bottom.

I adored plain, blonde Annie Faye, freckled face set off by a bowl hair cut, i.e., hair cut the same length, just below the ears, all the way around, save for the bangs. Annie made the first overture of friendship when we were in the fifth grade. One day she bought me ice cream (for a nickel) in our school cafeteria. In fact, she made this generous gesture numerous times. It sealed our friendship; I knew she liked me.

At her house I envied Annie her pet chihuahua, whom she lavishly kissed on the head and pampered. At our house, we weren't allowed the exorbitance, or foolishness as my farming relatives would contend, of retaining an indoor animal. (My parents made one exception. Because I fantasized about owning a parrot, having seen what fun one of my neighborhood friends had with hers, Mama consented to my getting a parakeet. Unfortunately one day–I was 9 years old at the time—I put him into a warm oven thinking it would cure him of what I had diagnosed as a cold. That actually did him in; I baked him to death.)

Not just her chihuahua but Annie and her older sister, Laura Sue, were pampered in their household. The girls' stepmother dressed the two siblings in expensive, sturdy, ready-made apparel. The Johnson sisters frequented beauty salons for their haircuts and styling, an expense my parents could ill afford. As a girl, I never went to (what we called then) a beautician to have my hair done. Mama cut, permed and styled our hair as well as her own. But the most obvious indication to me of the Johnson girls' wealth was the fact that Annie Faye and Laura Sue owned and wore jewelry, nice jewelry.

Annie's house rambled on, with three floors and at least ten spacious rooms. One of the latter was a recreation room in the basement that ran the length and half the width of the house where her dad exhibited his hunting trophies on the walls. Mr. Johnson, as some wealthy men still persisted in mid-twentieth century to do, annually hunted big game in the wilds of the western U. S. and in Alaska. After he returned from one of these week-long trips, he customarily took one of the animals he had bagged, such as a big horned sheep, elk, moose, or bear, to the taxidermist to have the head stuffed for mounting. I found the taxidermy both exotic and suffocating, creepily hanging all around over my head. A white fur rug with a head sticking up at one end, made from a polar bear Mr. Johnson had killed, claimed a place of honor on the rec room floor. When we played in the rec room or Annie threw a party and turned the lights down low, I avoided the glares emanating from the eyes of the dead menagerie.

Mr. Johnson parked his hunting trailer, when he wasn't using it, outside Annie's house in the driveway. He generously didn't object (at least not to my knowledge) to our playing inside his miniature, upscale house on wheels. In my childhood I had created all sorts of playhouses, ranging from a complex of exposed tree roots to sheet-covered chairs on the front porch, but never before had I encountered a preconstructed, real-life, opulent, fully-furnished playhouse as Mr. Johnson's trailer presented. We spent many happy hours of make-believe in that pinnacle of all my playhouses.

Another type of pretend that Annie and I relished was playing with paper dolls. I had been enamored with paper dolls since my preschool days when Aunt Olivia brought them home to me as a surprise. Annie and I most enjoyed movie star paper dolls such as Hedy Lamar, Ann Blythe, and Jane Powell. She and I would punch out the dolls and the doll clothes from our cardboard books and play with them all afternoon in her sunny, warm, large bedroom upstairs. Oftentimes our make-believe dialogue in the paper doll scenarios would strike us as hilarious, and we would giggle until tears rolled down our cheeks or one of us wet her pants. Because of such camaraderie, I loved Annie enormously and reveled in our friendship.

For a special treat when I spent the night at Annie's, we slept in an antique double bed in one of their traditionally formal, professionally decorated guest rooms. In the bed we took turns reading a book, preferably a mystery, aloud to each other until our eyelids grew heavy. One of our favorite mysteries was *Wild Dogs of Drowning Creek*.[1] We also took turns giving each other a back scratch, tickle, or rub—our version of the modern-day spa massage—before we went to sleep.

Many a time in the afternoons at the Johnsons' we played Clue because we preferred mysteries in a board game too. We liked to figure out "who dun it," how, and where: the butler in the kitchen with a knife? the colonel in the library with a candelabra? However, one of the greatest forms of entertainment at Annie's lay in her attic. There hung the collection of formal and semi-formal gowns Mrs. Johnson had purchased at rummage sales for the sole purpose of Annie's and Laura's playing dress-up. At our Miller household, we could never have imagined such treasure. For Annie and me, anticipatory socialization into female adulthood alternated, to a large extent, between the paper doll dialogues and acting out in the attic, donned in the lovely, sophisticated, secondhand gowns.

Compared to my house, another amazingly affluent occurrence at the Johnsons' was the elaborate Easter egg hunt to which Mrs. Johnson invited all Annie's and Laura Sue's friends. The hunt took place on their expansive, sloping, lush front lawn, a perfect setting for such a spring fete. All afternoon we ran around, tumbled, and with carefree laughter, ferreted out the brightly colored, plentiful eggs. As a reward for our endeavors, a banquet of Easter candy and pastries awaited us at the picnic table in the backyard. The treat I most savored was Mrs. Johnson's Lime Chocolate Delicious, a concoction of dry lime Jell-o whipped with evaporated milk until fluffy, poured into a crust of crushed chocolate wafers.

All was not paradise at the Johnsons', though. After Annie and I had become bosom buddies, her stepmother's bachelor brother came to live with the Johnson family. Annie revealed to me (Miss Goody-Good, of all people) that her step uncle requested that she, age 12 at the time, and Laura Sue, age 14, remove all their clothes and ride him piggy back, naturally in the seclusion of the girls' bedroom when their parents were absent. Even I knew something was wrong with that picture. But the uncle convinced the girls that his perversion was innocent fun that simply "made him feel good." The girls kindly complied with his wishes. Thus I learned about sexual abuse, although Annie swore her step uncle meant no harm. Shortly after Annie and I left elementary school, we parted ways, not because of the uncle incident per se but because of a combination of factors. In sum, Annie found me too immature, too naive. "Not cool" would be the contemporary expression to describe my state of psychological, physical, and social development as I approached puberty.

Before the watershed era of junior high, however, when I was in the 5th grade at Wasena I met my other closest friend in elementary school, Sammy Reynolds. Although different from Annie's, the action at Sammy's home proved equally exciting and experience enhancing. Sammy, cute as a button, small, with dark, short, curly hair, blue eyes and freckled face, was very bright and quite energetic. Before Sammy, his mother had given birth to twins who died. Older by the time Sammy came along, Mr. and Mrs. Reynolds doted on him, their last and only child.

I think Sammy considered me his sweetheart although my feelings towards him never went deeper than friendship. In hindsight, I would guess that the Reynolds encouraged the relationship between Sammy and me because they considered me a suitable companion, if not sister substitute, for their precious only child. I'm sure the Reynolds liked the fact that my parents expected us Miller children to adhere at all times to high moral standards; we attended church regularly and abided by the Ten Commandments and the Golden Rule. Mom and Dad taught us to be kind to all creatures great and small and to be scrupulously honest. We studied and worked diligently. Even during summers when we were out of school and too young to hold jobs, Dad wouldn't tolerate us kids sleeping in. A model student and only mildly extroverted, I was malleable yet intelligent, financially unspoiled, and perhaps most importantly, I always tried to please those around me–a perfect pal for Sammy Reynolds.

Socialization to please others was one of the basic tenets of rearing a little girl in the 1940s and 1950s. After all, role expectations of the era impelled females to be stay-at-home mothers and housewives, to be subordinate to their husbands, and to place their own wants and needs behind those of their family. This socialization process was sometimes subtle but always profound; I, for one, always tried to perform as others liked me to perform.

I tried to be the playmate the Reynolds wanted me to be for Sammy. Besides, I enjoyed visiting Sammy's house as much as Annie's. The Reynolds residence was nestled atop wooded hills in an upper class neighborhood of successful businessmen, professionals, and their families. In one of the homes down the street from the Reynolds, a psychiatrist had installed an elevator in his mansion. Not quite so opulent, Sammy's house was nonetheless an elegant, brick, three-story, commodious colonial, decorated beautifully with antiques, and included a two-car garage. Approximately an acre of well-manicured grass encircled the house. The yard dropped off steeply into woods in the back.

Once in a while Sammy and I watched the Reynolds' t.v., much larger than our newly acquired one at home. We most frequently viewed *Mr. Wizard*, a program starring one man who explained scientific phenomena and performed science experiments at a level comprehensible to young viewers. *Mr. Wizard* was Sammy's preference, not mine (we females were encouraged to avoid science; math too), but like a good little girl, I deferred to his choice. But Sammy and I cooked up more fun things to do than watch the box. Television in the 1950s offered limited programming; it was for the most part boring.

Sammy and I would head off to Mr. Reynolds' study in which his father kept his high-quality tape recorder, in those days typically a large, reel-to-reel, bulky instrument. In his munificence, Mr. Reynolds permitted Sammy and me to play with it. Left sitting on top of the desk, it was easy to operate and possessed an excellent tone quality. We derived endless hours of pleasure devising and taping our own talent shows; we sang, spun stories, and Sammy cracked jokes. Then for our prolonged entertainment and great mirth we played back everything we had recorded.

Down in one corner of the Reynolds' cavernous basement we often tinkered with Sammy's well-stocked chemistry set. Sammy conducted most of the experiments while I watched. The resulting bizarre smells, vivid colors, copious smoke, and minor explosions of Sammy's tinkering exhilarated us.

I dined at the Reynolds' home many times, a ritual quite different from eating at my house. To begin with, dinner at Sammy's house was much more peaceful than at ours. Although Dad frequently missed supper with us because he was on the road working, our family meals in the 1950s invariably included all three of us lively, talkative children. We Millers occasionally gave thanks for our food. We ate with mouths closed, used (paper) napkins, said "please" and "thank you," and following a relatively universal southern custom, often lingered at the table after having finished our meal. At the Reynolds' table, everyone behaved in a much more punctilious, mannerly fashion, beginning with the saying of grace while holding hands around the table. I felt a little awkward the first time I participated in this rite because I actually held Mr. Reynold's stub of an arm, not his hand, while we prayed. Mr. Reynolds had lost his left forearm and hand in an old hunting accident. It was unkindly rumored that he had purposely shot off his lower arm to avoid the draft in WWII.

At Sammy's we ate with expensive silver utensils and from china, with food served from bowls on the table (as opposed to being served from pots on the stove). Mrs. Reynolds kept a tablecloth and centerpiece on her table; table decor at our house would have severely taxed Mama's budget and energy. To protect her nice clothes, Mrs. Reynolds wore an apron while cooking; my mother seldom did. Mama didn't think it necessary: she possessed few, if any, expensive, dry-clean-only clothes. Mr. Reynolds presided over the table, often regaling us with didactic tales of the road to success. When done eating at Sammy's, we asked to be excused from the table. At our house when we had eaten our fill of supper and maybe sat for a few minutes, we exited the table without formality, in random order.

Sammy's parents not only invited me many times to their home, they also included me in family outings. Among those, I remember most vividly dining at Hotel Roanoke and at Natural Bridge. I felt shy and inept in the completely foreign milieu of these two classy hotel dining rooms. I don't remember our parents ever having taken us to a restaurant to eat. Most mid-twentieth century, lower-middle class families, with an average salary of under $5,000 couldn't afford such a luxury. Compare to 21st century prices, those in the mid-1950s appear ludicrously low ($10,000 for a modest new house, $1700-$2,000 for an automobile, 22-29 cents per gallon for gas, 17 cents for a loaf of bread, and 55 cents for a pound of hamburger) but for most families spending $1 per head at a nice eatery was too extravagant. As a family, we ate away from home only when we visited our relatives on holiday.

Terribly self-conscious at first with formal etiquette and table settings, I eventually grew a little more comfortable in that kind of environment. On one occasion, however, in the home of my friend, Alma Conner, I embarrassed myself at dinner. Mrs. Conner had prepared fried shrimp, replete with tails, for us. Never having eaten shrimp before, I proceeded at the evening meal to gnaw mine, starting with the tail. Naturally the family noticed my loud crunching; one member ventured to ask politely why I ate shrimp tails. Humiliated beyond belief as I then realized the aberration of eating the tails of shrimp, I immediately replied, "Oh, I always eat the tails at our house." Scraping my pride off the floor, I finished my helping of shrimp, laboriously grinding away at the tails.

I learned from the shrimp fiasco when in doubt, watch what everyone else is doing before making a move at the table. Thank heavens I never committed such a conspicuous faux pas when dining out with the Reynolds, although I'm certain they would've forgiven me and taught me better as well.

Twice the Reynolds treated me to dinner at the Hotel Roanoke. Not only did they introduce me to the courtly Regency Dining Room, but his parents let Sammy and me explore the hotel's reception room with the cloud-papered ceiling, the elegant ballrooms and powder rooms, and the inviting, capacious lobby, with its grand, antique oriental carpet and resplendent stone fireplace.

Less formal and renown than Hotel Roanoke, the Natural Bridge Hotel, 45 minutes north of Roanoke, nevertheless intimidated me, the eleven-year-old ingenue. The Reynolds, after I had somehow managed the decorum at lunch, introduced me to Natural Bridge itself. One of the seven natural modern wonders of the world, the bridge connects the top of two ridges. Below the bridge looms a great aperture created from eons of water cutting deeper and deeper into limestone. George Washington, as a young Virginia surveyor, purportedly carved his initials into one side of the towering earthen opening.

After lunch and the bridge, Sammy's parents took us for a swim in nearby Mountain Lake. I didn't actually swim; I played in the shallow water. I never learned to swim as a child because my father wouldn't allow us children ever to go swimming in a public pool. Dad feared our contracting polio. His was not an irrational fear; the whole nation was daily reminded in the newspaper, on the radio, and through first-hand accounts of the dangers of being stricken by the devastating disease. "Nineteen-fifty-two marked the worst polio year on record in the United States, with over 57,000 victims reported."[2] Imagining the specter of one of his children ending up in an airtight, claustrophobic iron lung or at the very least crippled like Franklin Delano Roosevelt, not only did he forbid us to swim, but my father also required us to lie down and rest every afternoon during the summer. No preventive medicine for polio existed for me and my cohorts; avoidance of fatigue and crowds was believed our only hope. Although Dr. Jonas E. Salk's inoculation for polio was administered to roughly two million elementary school children all over the United States for the first time in1954, the vaccine was not declared universally safe until 1955 when I was almost 13 years old.[3]

Poliomyelitis prevailed as the scourge of the U.S. in the 1940s and '50s. My parents remembered all too well how in 1944 polio wrought death, panic, and havoc in the small furniture factory town of Hickory, a close neighbor of North Wilkesboro, in the Catawba River Valley of rural North Carolina. Over 400 people from the Catawba Valley, most of whom were children, were rushed to Memorial Hospital in nearby Charlotte, as well as to other local hospitals, to be treated. When the hospital ran out of beds, army tents were set up on the lawn to accommodate the onslaught of polio patients. Iron lungs and medical personnel were flown in. *Life* Magazine described the situation as follows: "Youngsters with painful, useless limbs, some unable to swallow or scarcely able to breathe, they came from mining villages up in the hills, mill towns in the valley, from outlying farms and urban centers."[4] Outsiders shunned Hickory, referred to as Polio City in the newspapers, for fear of contracting the polio virus. Within Hickory itself, virtually all public places such as theaters and libraries closed down, and citizens drove through their town with car windows rolled up, even on the hottest days.[5]

In the summer of 1953, however, the well-informed and rationally minded Reynolds allowed Sammy and me to play in Mountain Lake. Knowing that the lake was continually replenished with fresh water and that the number of tourists in the lake was minimal at that time, Sammy's parents considered the danger of our contracting polio unlikely or nil. Whatever the case, from splashing around in the cold water too long I succumbed to a chill that would not abate. The Reynolds scurried me out of the water, wrapped me in a blanket, and rushed me back home. It was not the last time the Reynolds had to deal with my physical fragility.

The next time I managed a dismal finish to a Reynolds' bash occurred in quite a different setting, that of a formal dance. Ultimately for Sammy's benefit but still a gift for me, Mrs. Reynolds provided me a very special opportunity of taking ballroom dancing. I loved to dance but my parents never gave me dancing lessons; they couldn't afford tap or ballet classes, and, they thought that my tumor-ridden knee, discovered by the time I was 10, would preclude pursuit of that kind of physical activity. Yet they let me attend the ballroom sessions with Sammy. Although not referred to at the time as ballroom dancing or junior cotillion preparation, the lessons Sammy and I took were tantamount to both. Escorted by Mrs. Reynolds, Sammy and I for months persevered in the weekly dance classes at the downtown YWCA. Along with ballroom dance etiquette we mostly practiced the box step waltz. Lessons culminated in the night of the big formal dance. We dolled up in our finest. Mrs. Reynolds somehow had produced for me to wear, a blue chiffon, floor-length gown, with a softly ruffled, slightly scooped neck. Sweet in its simplicity, the gown was decorated only with a narrow, black velvet waist ribbon with a small blue chiffon rose attached to one side. Sammy and I thoroughly enjoyed our evening, that is until almost time to leave. I had so vigorously polkaed that I became nauseous. Once again Mrs. Reynolds and Sammy rushed me home. We arrived at my house in the nick of time. I threw open our front door, ran straight through the kitchen to our first floor bathroom and regurgitated into the toilet.

Interestingly, Sammy never complained about my physical foibles, but once we left elementary school, the friendship between Sammy and me quickly dissipated, just as it had between Annie and me.

NOTES

1. *Wild Dogs of Drowning Creek* numbers just one of the 80 books Manly Wade Wellman wrote in his lifetime, from 1903 to 1986. Neither Annie nor I at the time we read his book knew that the author resided in Chapel Hill, N.C., and that many of his

adventure stories are set in the mountains of North Carolina, my home state. What's more, Wellman's popular Silver John series are based on the history and folklore of the Appalachian region. One literary historian predicts that Wellman's book, *Who Fears the Devil?*, will still be read 100 years from now. It is most ironic for me that Wellman's book title is reflective of a major theme in this present work, "fear," and that it poses a pertinent question for this author in the face of her grandmother's indoctrination.

   2. Oshinsky, 161.
   3. Oshinsky, 189, and O'Neill, 136
   4. "Infantile Paralysis," *Life*, 25-28.
   5. Oshinsky, 69-72.

SUGGESTED READINGS

Davis, J. Lee. *Bits of History and Legends around and about the Natural Bridge of Virginia, from 1730 to 1950.* Lynchburg, Va.: Natural Bridge of Virginia, Inc., 1949.

"Infantile Paralysis." *Life* Magazine. (31 July 1944): 25-28.

The Natural Bridge: An Ancient Natural Wonder in Virginia's Shenandoah Valley. Historic Landmark and Nature Park, Caverns, Monacan Indian Village, Hotel. Natural Bridge: Natural Bridge of Virginia, 2005.

O'Neill, William L. *American High: Confident Years 1945-1960.* New York: The Free Press, 1986.

Oshinsky, David M. *Polio: An American Story.* Oxford, N.Y.: Oxford UP, 2005.

Seavey, Nina Gilden, Jane S. Smith, and Paul Wagner. *A Paralyzing Fear: The Triumph over Polio in America.* New York: TV Books, 1998.

Wellman, Manly Wade. *Wild Dogs of Drowning Creek.* New York: Holiday House, 1952.

Chapter Seven

Repression in the Bible Belt

As a youngster I walked the straight and narrow. The combination of my grandmother Miller's fundamentalist indoctrination, parental insistence upon exemplary behavior, explicit religious guidance (always Christian) in school, censorship of lurid programming in the media, my constancy to the church, and living in non-cosmopolitan, conservative, southern Bible Belt communities not only clinched my uprightness but insulated my universe.

High religiosity and churchgoing in the United States characterized the years coinciding with my childhood. "In 1948 a poll found that 95 percent of respondents believed in God and 90 percent prayed to Him."[1] By 1955, when 49% of the American population claimed they attended church regularly, church-going reached its zenith.[2] In our community, families who didn't worship in church were considered low class; only good-for-nothing parents allowed their children to stay abed on Sunday mornings. None but the most deviant, belligerent souls publicly declared themselves agnostics, let along atheists. The word "atheism" was hardly uttered, at least not in our social circles. During the 1940s and '50s the United States unquestionably qualified as a nation of God-fearing believers, so much so that in 1954 "under God" was added to the pledge of allegiance to the flag and "In God We Trust" appeared on all U.S. coinage. Every morning in public school, classes began with prayer and a Bible reading, after which we recited the pledge to the flag. Media, including motion pictures, reflected great respect for religion, especially Christian beliefs and morals. (Witness the popular series of movies–*The Bells of St. Mary's* [1945] for one–starring the crooner Bing Crosby as a charismatic Catholic priest.) Neither did people take God's name in vain, not publicly anyway.

Both my nuclear and extended families placed great importance on religion and what they deemed Christian behavior. While my grandmother espoused a primitive Baptist theology, my parents, thank God, took a more moderate approach to religion. Yet when my nuclear family moved away from Grandmother and Cricket, I never seemed to escape her religious angst in which malignant spirits held great sway. Despite the damage to my psyche from Grandmother's religious legacy, church remained an integral part of my young life, as was the case for millions of young folks in the '40s and '50s.[3]

In Roanoke we soon joined Raleigh Court Methodist Church, close to our Wasena neighborhood. The Methodists enjoyed a much more liberal, educated clergy and congregation than did Grandmother's Primitive Baptist one. Most of the time, then, churchgoing proved innocuous enough for me, and even rational and pleasant. My sister, Pat, and I regularly trotted off to Sunday School and MYF (Methodist Youth Fellowship). I grew quite fond of my Sunday School teacher at Raleigh Court, a lovely, sweet, older mother figure and female role model named Mrs. Cartwright.

MYF met on Sunday evenings. At one such meeting I, obviously not at the moment daunted by fear of fiery retribution, embarrassed my sister (and ultimately myself) by pulling the chair out from under her as she tried to sit down. Our peers, seated in a big circle in Fellowship Hall, witnessed the spectacle of Pat landing on her rump, skirt askew. Identifying with my sister's humiliation, not only Pat but most of the already self-conscious adolescents blushed at the sight. Certainly I blushed. I felt truly ashamed for having committed such an obnoxious prank. I don't know what possessed me; I guess that little devil Grandmother had tried so hard to exorcize in me came out on that occasion.

In Roanoke I didn't completely escape from the Baptist Church either. Our neighbors, the Sanders, a particularly good-looking and sophisticated family, invited me to go to Vacation Bible School with their children one summer. They belonged to an upscale Baptist church in a ritzy neighborhood of South Roanoke. Mama was only too happy to have me accompany them because she always approved of religious education and of her offspring socializing with what she considered nice people. During that Bible School episode I began a life-long romance with sub-Saharan Africa. It just so happened that the church's missionary to Africa had returned to the States and was sharing her experiences in our Bible School sessions. I took one look at the photos of her holding a tiny African baby on her lap, surrounded by other children against a tropical backdrop, and at her cowry beads and other artifacts, and I was hooked.

Another one of the most affecting encounters with religion for me as a child took place one street over from Howbert Avenue where we lived. This street, Wasena Avenue, borrowed its name from the general neighborhood area. There, in a brick house very similar to ours–two-storied with a front porch, and inside, a large foyer with steps off to the right leading upstairs–I babysat for a little boy named Bernard. I adored Bernard, less than a year old when I began sitting him. I especially enjoyed cuddling him and rocking him to sleep. Encouraged to babysit, both to earn money and to gain experience for our pre-ordained female role in life, i.e., mother, many girls my age (pre-pubescent) and I were great little babysitters, quite nurturing, conscientious, reliable, and cheap (at the going rate of 50 cents an hour).

Also in that house, in her large foyer, Bernard's mother held Bible School one day a week after public school hours for neighborhood kids. I started attending her Bible School sessions. Along with at least a half dozen other kids, I sat quietly and attentively in a circle of chairs lining the walls of the foyer. A gifted story-teller, she captivated us with her larger than life Bible tales, e.g., those of Joseph and his coat of many colors and David the giant slayer. She illustrated her stories with colorful paper Biblical figures, backed with felt, which adhered to a large, flannel covered easel. At each session she handed out weekly Bible verses typed on heavy, colored construction paper in different shapes. If we memorized those verses by the next week when we met, we received a gold star on her honors poster. We not only learned Bible stories and verses, but we also committed to memory the books of the Bible. As an added attraction, Bernard's mother served us refreshments: cookies and Kool-Aid. (None of us would've predicted the bad rap Jim Jones gave Kool-Aid and religious commitment decades later.)

My days of neighborhood Bible School ended the spring before I started junior high school. My sister and I severed our membership at Raleigh Court Methodist too when in 1954 we moved across town from Wasena. We never drove back to our old community to attend church. In those days, commuting across town for church-going or anything else wasn't a reasonable option; driving that kind of distance was too expensive, in terms of both gasoline and time. Most middle-class mothers had too many household duties and too many children to care for to chauffeur more than absolutely necessary. Besides, most families owned only one car; if the father needed the car, the mother and the children had to do without wheels, and vice-versa. Always the penurious family, we joined a church, Huntington Court Methodist, on Williamson Road, within a couple of miles from our new home.

At our new church, Pat and I again attended Sunday School and Methodist Youth Fellowship meetings. Over time I held various offices in MYF, eventually becoming president. Some of the most fun times I experienced from my pubescent years on through high school involved MYF activities; for example, going to church camp in Blackstone, Virginia, where my girlfriends and I met new Methodist boyfriends and stole kisses behind the bushes. An especially wonderful event for us boys and girls took the form of an MYF planning retreat where we spent the weekend in a cabin at the foot of Mount Rogers in Virginia.[4] Once there, our activities ranged from planning upcoming MYF programs, hiking up Mt. Rogers, picnicking on top of the mountain with s'-mores for dessert (in case the reader hails from another planet, a s'more is a luscious contrivance of toasted marshmallows and a Hershey's milk chocolate bar sandwiched between two graham crackers), to dancing the night away on the outdoor deck of the cabin (unlike strict Southern Baptists, Methodists dance without compunction).

My sister and I participated in a variety of other church activities during our early adolescence. For instance, annually for Lent, we ate a sacrificial super, consisting of a single, unadorned baked potato for each individual, intended to teach us about hunger and suffering. Also each year our youth Sunday School classes traveled to Natural Bridge for Easter sunrise service. Upon arrival in the early morning dark, we hiked a short distance down to the bridge where bleachers had been set up for those attending the function. A volunteer church choir provided glorious resurrection music, and a visiting minister preached the Easter story. All this transpired under a natural canopy of dew-laden woods while the sun slowly rose in the background. Some Easter Sundays dawned pretty chilly for the new spring finery we girls wore, light-weight dresses replete with color-coordinated gloves, high heels, and new hats. Too vain and foolish to wear wraps, we suffered cold just to show off our new outfits.

Before Pat and I learned to sew our own clothes, Mama made lovely Easter dresses for us. One of my girlfriends so loved the red dotted Swiss dress that Mama fashioned for me when I was thirteen that she talked about it for years afterward as the prettiest dress she'd ever seen. Very striking, the transparent, dotted outer fabric of the dress overlay a solid red sheath with spaghetti straps. Too fancy for any of my other youthful activities, the dress never saw any wear save for church.

For my generation what a girl wore to church and elsewhere mattered a great deal. After all, clothes reflected a girl's self-image and her ability to attract a male, the latter our most important endeavor in life, or so we were led to believe. Nevertheless, for me, church affairs carried greater import than wardrobe.

One of the things that bothered me most as a church-going child, especially by the time I was old enough to pay attention to segregation issues, was that our congregation remained staunchly white. Ostensibly the most Christian of all social institutions, the church upheld exclusion and, in essence, practiced racism. In my youth at Huntington Court Church I proposed a joint activity, it didn't matter to me what kind, for our MYF group and our counterpart from a black Methodist church in town. Although our MYF members supported an integrated youth session, our Director of Christian Education sponsor, of whom we were quite fond and who usually always went to bat for us, and other adult mentors in the church squashed my idea. They argued that too many church members would find such a plan offensive, if not outrageous. In other words, the congregation would not break away from the normative segregation patterns in our community and town.

The church exerted such a strong influence over us that it largely curtailed any socially unacceptable behavior on our part. In grade school, we looked upon smoking and drinking as immoral. In junior high and high school most of us suppressed sexual desire, that is if we recognized it, with a vengeance; a little voice would go off in us girls' heads reminding us that if we became pregnant, we might as well be dead. Needless to say, we never heard of marijuana. "Nothing like the drug culture of the 1960s existed anywhere in the United States in the 1950s. . . ."[5] Yet we and our houses of worship condoned obliviousness to the cruelty we inflicted, intentionally or not, upon certain members in our community, because of their race or ethnicity.

Growing up, my friends and I seldom encountered anyone "of color," although the Miller family claimed among its members a Mexican American. When my Uncle Clarence was stationed in El Paso during WWII, he met and married Helen, a sweet, genteel woman of Mexican descent. After the war Clarence brought Aunt Helen back to Winston-Salem where they both found employment. We didn't often have the pleasure of Helen's company although she and Uncle Clarence visited North Wilkesboro on occasion. I have two salient memories of Helen, now long deceased. I recall one time when Helen showed up at Grandmother Miller's house with white splotches on her face. Curious, I asked Mama why Helen had spots on her face. Mama sadly replied that Helen in an effort to make her face whiter had scrubbed it with a scouring compound containing bleach; by lightening her skin, she hoped to better blend into the WASP community of which she was now a part. On another of her visits Aunt Helen shared with us photos of a party her family honored her with on her sixteenth birthday. The photo showed her and all her female kin garbed in beautiful, flowing white evening gowns, the male relations wearing white tuxedos, and a string quartet standing off to one side. My mother commented on the irony that while Helen no doubt endured prejudice from some of the anglos with whom she interacted in North Carolina, her socioeconomic background was superior to most of theirs.

As I grew older, I began to more clearly understand why Helen had attempted to lighten her face. Still, the terms "minority group" or "ethnic group" were unknown in my vocabulary and in that of my friends. Minority relations was not an issue, certainly not a public one, in the town of Roanoke in the 1950s. It's not that our town didn't incorporate any ethnicities besides white Anglo-Saxon; it was more the case that minorities maintained a low profile and whites contentedly acceded to that state of affairs. In Roanoke such minorities as Greeks, Lebanese, Catholics and Jews were among those groups who looked white but who didn't broadcast their respective cultures vis-a-vis the WASP world. As a little girl, I heard now and then only vague references to Jewish affiliation; for example, someone mentioned in passing that Shapiro was a Jewish name, or a beautiful little classmate of mine told me she took Yiddish lessons after school.

Much later in my life, Greek friends related a story to me that in the 1940s when they as children wanted their mother to take them to Lakeside, a local amusement park in Roanoke, they would be admitted only if she kept her mouth shut. In other words, the children spoke English well and appeared to be white Anglo-Saxon, so they had no trouble getting into, and staying at, the park, but if their mother was overheard speaking Greek, they all would have been denied access.

From the same Greek friends I learned that their parents, despite their economic prosperity, were barred in the 1950s from purchasing a house in an upper-class white neighborhood in Roanoke. One of the means through which WASPs disallowed members of specific ethnic groups from buying houses in certain residential areas was the restrictive covenant clause. These clauses, incorporated in many deeds to homes, stated either which groups were prohibited from purchasing a piece of real estate or to which group the purchaser was restricted.[6] Another real estate practice called steering prevented minorities from residing in areas they could otherwise afford and/or most desired. In steering, an agent never showed houses for sale in upper-class neighborhoods to people he (real estate agents were almost exclusively male in Roanoke at that time) even suspected of being non-WASP. If a potential buyer spoke with an accent over the phone to a real estate agent, the latter immediately categorized the individual as a minority and would arrange to show homes to him/her only in minority neighborhoods.

Although in our small southern community we all lived mostly segregated lives, particularly in our places of worship and in our neighborhoods, there were some exceptions. A case in point, an affable young Lebanese man and his darling WASP wife lived next door to us when we moved across town from Wasena to the Williamson Road area. Too, when we still lived in Wasena, a Catholic family moved in and remained across the street, without any protests or snide remarks from neighbors. The thirtyish, attractive, and extroverted parents sent their three children, all rosy-cheeked Irish, bouncy and smiley, to the private Catholic school in downtown Roanoke. Both the school buildings and the adjoining august St. Andrews Cathedral commanded a hilltop, in the midst of a sizeable, mostly poor, black neighborhood below.

When urban renewal programs swept the U.S. during the 1950s, many black homes in close proximity to St. Andrews were demolished.[7] In the old Gainsboro neighborhood west of Williamson Road where the cathedral stands, 452 homes were razed by 1956.[8] St. Andrews still stands salient on the Roanoke City center landscape, listed in the national registry of historic buildings and proudly touted as a hometown treasure, while many vibrant black neighborhoods disappeared with no fanfare whatsoever. Urban renewal agendas readily took precedence over traditional black community cohesion. Another case in point: the Roanoke Civic Center complex now stands on the ground where an 83-acre black neighborhood once existed.[9]

In the 1950s in Roanoke, blacks, referred to as Negroes in polite society, represented the most populous minority. The racial situation in our town was analogous to that described by Ralph Ellison in *Invisible Man* (1952), wherein the average white person rarely contemplated or acknowledged a black person. With the exception of the old black laborer on Grandpa Church's farm, I never interacted with a black person until after I reached adulthood. We were aware of the existence of black neighborhoods, but such areas were, consciously or not, avoided by whites. To and from home, work, school, church or entertainment, whites bypassed those neighborhoods whenever possible. Except in the case of menial black labor, such as black maids working in wealthy white households, the paths of those in the black community seldom crossed that of the whites. Black neighborhoods filled out-of-the-way, geographically undesirable (such as near the railroad tracks) nooks and crannies of the city.

Blacks shared no public facilities or institutions with whites in the 1950s in Roanoke. Although in 1952 the city boasted "the finest Negro high school in Virginia," Lucy Addison, Roanoke did not integrate its schools until the fall of 1960, the fall after I had graduated high school.[10] Equipped later with a college degree, I briefly taught in public school with Mr. Chubb, a black colleague and dear friend of mine. He told me he never learned to swim because he had no place in Roanoke as a child to go to learn or practice. He also told me his family vacations consisted of joining other black friends and/or family members on land out in the country owned by them privately. Far from the view of whites, out of harm's way, they ate and slept in their own trailers parked on their land. (Mr. Chubb, deservedly so, years later became principal of an elementary school in Roanoke.)

Aside from the egregious, debilitating effects of segregation, incidents of physical violence against blacks in our community were rare, or more likely, rarely reported because they were not deemed significant to whites. I do recall stories, though, of obstreperous, delinquent white boys throwing eggs on streets and cars in black neighborhoods or driving through in search of a vulnerable individual whom they could torment with hateful words or spiteful tomfoolery. Prejudice and discrimination against blacks lay indelibly in the collective consciousness of our southern community. When I was growing up it was not uncommon to hear, I'm ashamed to say, the derogatory appellation "nigger." Deeply embedded in the southern vernacular, such aspersion greatly troubled me then as it does now.

NOTES

1. O'Neill, 212.
2. Noll, 476.
3. Membership in the Methodist church grew more in that era than it had since the 1920s; the Catholic church baptized millions of babies; the Southern Baptist congregation grew by multiple thousands; and enrollment in Jewish and Protestant seminaries doubled previous numbers (Catholic seminary enrollment increased as well). Noll, 437.
4. Graebner, 119.
5. Mohlenbrock, 72.
6. During his administration President Truman at least banned restrictive covenants in all federally insured housing. O'Neill, 103.
7. These urban renewal programs translated through imminent domain into the displacement of the urban poor into even less visible, impoverished neighborhoods or into government subsidized housing projects. The latter, populated at first with almost exclusively dispossessed, poor blacks, sprang up rather quickly in numerous locations in Roanoke City.
8. White, 115.
9. White, 115.
10. White, 114.

SUGGESTED READINGS

Ahlstrom, Sydney E. *A Religious History of the American People*. New Haven, Conn.: Yale UP, 1972.

Ellison, Ralph. *Invisible Man*. New York: Random House, 1952.

Graebner, William. *Coming of Age in Buffalo*. Philadelphia: Temple UP, 1990.

Grossman, James K. *Black Southerners and the Great Migration*. Chicago: University of Chicago Press, 1989.

Hornsby, Alton. *Chronology of African-American History from 1942 to the Present*. 2nd ed. Detroit: Gale Research, 1997.

Mohlenbrock, Robert H. "Mt. Rogers, Virginia (Jefferson National Forest)." *Natura History* 11 (December 1990): 72-73.

Noll, Mark A. *A History of Christianity in the United States and Canada*. Grand Rapids, Mich.: William B. Eerdmans Publishing Company, 1992.

O'Neill, William L. *American High: Confident Years 1945-1960*. New York: The Free Press, 1986.

White, Clare. *Roanoke 1740-1982*. Roanoke, Va.: Hickory Printing, 1982.

Chapter Eight

Vexatious Pubescence

In 1954 during the summer after I finished elementary school, my sister and her best friend, Cherise, oriented me (not intentionally, of course) to the adolescent world which lay ahead. They took me to a favorite teenage hang-out at the time, Robert's swimming pool off Brandon Road in southwest Roanoke. I suspect my mother made Pat take me along; I can't imagine Pat wanting the company of her odious little sister amongst her peers. Regardless, I loved going to the pool, but not because of the swimming–I couldn't swim a lick. What delighted me was the ambiance. Incessant, loud rock and roll music, first and foremost "Shake, Rattle, and Roll" by Bill Haley and the Comets, set the tone for the outing by the pool.[1] Lots of teenagers — whose (seemingly) savoir faire, conversations and interactions enthralled me — populated the pool side. Too, I looked in awe upon my sister and beautiful Cherise with their perfectly proportioned bodies shown off in their one-piece, strapless bathing suits (modest in comparison to today's string bikinis), their clean-shaven legs, and their feigned aloofness to boys.

Unfortunately, the swimming pool orientation to teenage life did little to help me fit in at Woodrow Wilson Junior High School where I entered in the fall. My old elementary school friends, also now at Woodrow, had more or less abandoned me; we were choosing different directions in our struggle to grow up. My elementary school popularity long gone and forgotten, I retained my little girl's physique, personified the goody-good, and felt unsure of who I was.

In my new school I tried to emulate the stylishly dressed girls, with their "uniforms" of pull-over sweaters worn with calf-length, straight, form-fitting skirts. Standard footwear consisted of bobby socks and saddle oxfords for casual dress and for dress-up occasions, flat heeled, black leather Capezios worn with sheer nylon hose. A garter belt, looking and feeling like a medieval torture device, held up the nylons. As the recipient of the hand-me-down garments of my curvaceous older sister, I in my attempts at modish conformity succeeded mainly in accentuating my skinny, underdeveloped body. Thank goodness Pat's shoes were way too big for me, or I would've looked even more the pathetic clown.

Other than school letting out early one day in the fall of 1954 because of the deluge from Hurricane Hazel, my most salient recollections of Woodrow Junior High School evoke self-mortification of one kind or another due to my lack of maturity, both physically and socially.[2] I epitomized the ingenue in the midst of teenage sexual curiosity, experimentation, and hormonal explosions. At one sock hop when I was dancing the dirty shag, because it was the latest dance craze in the South and because I so loved to dance, I couldn't quite understand why cat calls emanated from some on-lookers. We referred to the shag as "dirty" because of the way we danced solo, bending our knees while twisting our hips from side-to-side, and slithered slowly towards our partners who faced us. (The original shag of Myrtle Beach, S.C., consists of fancy footwork and complex turns; in no way does it resemble our swivel-hipped motions in the 1950s.) I would've blushed profusely and left the floor had I realized the full sexual implications of my body movements. I just considered myself a darn good dancer. Likewise, I didn't have a clue as to the fascination of my peers with cigarettes and beer, the perennially popular adolescent contraband. Always the sheltered little girl, I never drank or smoked (with the exception of the garage incident with my cousin way back in Cricket, N.C.) until my first fraternity party in college.

In junior high (and later high school) sock hops intoxicated me, though. I reveled in them. The term "sock hop" arose from dances being held in the school gymnasium where shoes had to be removed to preserve the smooth, athletic surface of the gym floor. Before entering the dance, we all dutifully took off our shoes and threw them into a pile near the entrance. For our Friday night gym dances we gyrated in our socks to the latest pop music on 45-speed records spun by professional DJs. Sometimes our school allowed hops during lunch periods. At those, usually a student who possessed an extensive record collection and who was thoroughly versed in the top billboard songs played disc jockey. After having eaten, students went in and danced for about 10 or 15 minutes until they had to hustle to their next classes. The frantic retrieval of shoes after the lunch hops resembled bedlam.

Besides sock hops, I enjoyed changing classes, a nice turnaround from the grade school system of staying in the same room all day. My good fortune in having gifted teachers continued into junior high. I idolized my young, attractive home room/history teacher at Woodrow, Mrs. McDonald. Not only did she impart to us her expertise in American history, but she made it come alive in a way most teachers can never achieve. She acted out characters and events from the past with remarkable energy and humor. An exquisitely dressed live wire, she was captivating to watch in every way.

I considered my violin teacher, Mr. David Tyler, pretty special too. My violin lessons, begun while still in elementary school as part of my parents' plan to provide me a skill in case I should lose a leg to bone cancer, carried on into seventh grade with Mr. Tyler. Tall, thin David, with his fiery red, unruly long hair, appeared the stereotypic mad musician, but "mad" he was not. He played professionally in the Roanoke Symphony. This delightful, talented young man unfailingly demonstrated great patience with me when my ear-splitting screeching betrayed a gross lack of practice. More importantly, he won the hearts of my parents the first time he came to our home to give me a lesson. Then and there, at Mom and Dad's request, he demonstrated with great zeal how a country fiddlin' tune could be played on a violin. We all admired the versatility of this classically trained musician, not to mention his willingness to let his hair down.

Soon after Woodrow, I began taking private lessons from David at his house located across town because halfway through my first year in junior high, the Miller family moved again, close to the Tylers' neighborhood.[3] Each week when I went to Mr. Tyler's house after school for a lesson, his darling, dainty spouse and their cat, Egghead, cheerfully greeted me at their door. Both David and his wife treated me as a daughter.

Regardless of the continued music lessons with my adored teacher, the unexpected move to northwest Roanoke for us Millers dramatically changed my school and social situations. In the first place, our parents had planned to move us all back to North Wilkesboro. Familiar with Dad's expertise in lumber, a newly founded super home store in North Wilkesboro had asked him to come back and work for them. Although Dad accepted their offer only on a trial basis, we were pretty certain we'd be moving back to Carolina. Dad took a leave of absence from Associated Transport, went back to his home town, and left us in Roanoke to prepare to follow him. We were surprised when after only a few months Dad returned for good to Roanoke and to his trucking job. Dad's explanation for not staying with the super home store? He said, "I've never before dealt with such a bunch of crooks." That's my dad–scrupulously honest.

In anticipation of our move back to North Carolina, my friends had thrown a going-away party for me. Interestingly, after having readied themselves for my departure and said their farewells, they seemed angry and disillusioned by my remaining in Roanoke. Part of this I'm sure was due to their having prepared themselves emotionally for my leave-taking only to find out I was staying. For another, at the going-away party, I, still a foolish child, unthinkingly alienated some of my girlfriends by flirting too much with the boys and in turn annoyed the boys with my promiscuous coquettish behavior. To add to the above, some of my friends had given me going-away presents and felt it only fair under the circumstances to have them returned. Finally, they questioned the Miller family credibility in announcing plans.

Meanwhile we had put our house on Howbert Avenue up for sale. As luck would have it, it sold almost immediately, forcing Mom and Dad to find another home rather quickly. To be closer to Associated Transport and to save Mama from the relatively long drive she often made in the middle of the night to take Dad to work, our parents decided to relocate from the well-established southwest section of Roanoke to the newer northwest Williamson Road residential area.

Young and grossly uninformed, I was unfamiliar with Williamson Road, probably the single most well-known street in Roanoke. In the early 1950s Williamson Road constituted the first true urban sprawl, commercial strip of our town. Small businesses, including a variety of restaurants and motels, had established themselves on both sides of Williamson, starting past Hotel Roanoke downtown and running north all the way out to Hollins Road (Rt. 11), a distance of 8 miles altogether. I might've been more excited about moving to the area had I realized that the approximately 3-mile segment of Williamson that ran from Orange Avenue north to Hershberger Road maintained a reputation as the favorite cruising strip for teenage drivers. Adolescents also liked all the hamburger joints (not to be mistaken for the famous fast-food burger chains which were founded later: MacDonald's in 1955, Hardee's in 1960, and Wendy's in 1969) along the thoroughfare, especially the drive-in restaurants such as Toot's, where they could show off their cars, their dates, or order french fries curbside.[4]

About a mile off Williamson Road, roughly halfway between Roanoke City center and Hollins Road, Dad bought us a brand new, small brick home on Tenth Street Extension (inexorably, we moved to the street with the same name of the one I had walked upon so timorously with my grandmother in North Wilkesboro). Although we were generally happy with the house, it didn't quite measure up to the American belief that anything new is better. In the first place, it sat along a street with much more traffic than on Howbert. Second, it had the same number of rooms as our old habitat on Howbert, yet it came with only one bathroom as compared to our former domicile which included one full- and one half-bath. (Dad often remarked that it was a good thing that he traveled so much in his work because of the great difficulty of competing with four females for the use of the sole bathroom in our old house.) On the other hand, the brand new Tenth Street structure evinced a thorough cleanliness impossible to achieve in an older, more worn home. Additionally, the new full basement held out promise for a sizeable, finished recreation room, a most desirable feature in a modern dwelling, especially one in which teenagers resided. (Dad, working alone and spouting expletives, did soon build us a rec room extending one whole side of the basement.)

In keeping with the contemporary style of our new house, my parents splurged on modern living room furniture, the first they had purchased in my memory. The sleek, low slung, upholstered forest green couch and two chairs rested on shiny, hardwood floors. The couch faced the voguish picture window across the room. Mama embellished the window with contemporary, heavy, ceiling-to-floor, draw-drapes depicting diminutive woods with deer. Illogically, however, our wide, paneless window, a must-have feature of any up-to-date abode, looked out onto the busy street and the home on the other side rather than the suburban countryside it was designed to picture.

The house sat on about a half acre completely devoid of trees; only some newly planted shrubs abutting the front of the house supplied foliage to the yard. Recently seeded with grass, the backyard left plenty of room for Mama's eventual strawberry patch and for her clothesline. My mother, as was the case for the majority of middle-class American housewives in the early 1950s, did not own a clothes dryer (and, in fact, Mama still wrestled with her wringer type washing machine when we first moved to Tenth Street). She laboriously hung her clean clothes outdoors to withstand the elements, including temperatures ranging from extreme hot to extreme cold in our Roanoke Valley climate. Even given a sunny day—which helped to accelerate bleaching and outdoor drying—defecating birds, rusty clothes pins, and rowdy children always jeopardized clean laundry and, hence, frustrated housewives.

In our new house, Pat and I shared bedrooms on separate sides of our good-sized finished attic, so large it would qualify today as a great room (a term we weren't familiar with then). It was divided in the middle at the front by an enclosed staircase ascending from the first floor and situated directly across a minuscule foyer at the entrance of our home. A door to the staircase provided us privacy from those entering through our front door. In the summertime we sweltered in that upstairs bedroom despite Dad's efforts of installing a fan in the window in each end. The other factor besides the temperature that I wasn't happy with in our shared space was Pat's habit of listening to music on her dinky radio every night while I was trying to fall asleep. During the school year I was particularly grateful that the popular music station WROV at least signed off the air at midnight (with the song, "Goodnight, My Love"), a common practice for our local radio stations in the 1950s.[5] Only then was I able to sleep soundly. The one perk upstairs was our walk-in closet, occupying a gable space originally designed for a second bathroom; we opted to use it for a closet instead. Not incredibly spacious, the walk-in nevertheless accommodated our modest wardrobes and outsized by far the closets in the rest of our house, as well as those standard in the average lower-middle class home of that era.

Compared to our former one, our Tenth Street Extension neighborhood was newer, having been established decades later than Wasena. Ironically, however, one of our favorite features in the new hood was an old-fashion mom-and-pop store just around the corner from our house. Instead of walking around the corner, though, we easily accessed the store by cutting diagonally across our backyard and that of our neighbor's. This short cut enabled us to get to the store in about three minutes, a trek we made countless times. The store consisted of only one rather dimly lit room, but it was jam-packed with a variety of canned goods, such as vegetables and fruits, and with household staples such as coffee, boxed cereal, milk and bread. Seasonal fresh fruits, tomatoes, for instance, were available too. Of course, we kids gravitated to the goodies found on or close by the counter–the candy, soft drinks, cakes, and cookies. The mild-mannered, soft-spoken, sole operator-owner of the store rendered a good male role model for us kids as he waited on all customers, big or small, old or young, with courtesy and infinite patience.

Another positive role model, this one female and elderly, lived beside us in the house on the corner. With her regal, genteel manner Mrs. Circle commanded respect from young and old alike. The long-time widow of a college president and the epitome of the Southern Lady, she never raised her literate voice or uttered profanity. She never compromised her elegance either, even when she paid my baby sister, Angela, to routinely rub moisture cream on the dried-up skin of her back where she couldn't reach.

On the other side of us resided a charming young couple, Joey, of Lebanese descent, and his Anglo wife, Dedie, both of whom we adored. In the summer Dedie spent an inordinate amount of time lying in the sun, toasting her skin until she acquired a dark suntan. In those days, adolescents viewed a dark tan as cool; we actively worked on deeply tanning our skin, the darker the more hip. (It's fascinating that so many people in American culture have devalued genetically dark skin while at the same time greatly admired suntanned skin.) In between days of basking in the sun, Dedie also taught my mom how to make a delectable Lebanese lamb pastry.

Joey made his living from having taken over his parents' combination mom-and-pop store and club/bar in a black neighborhood several miles from our neighborhood. Quite late one night Joey invited me and my girlfriend–we happened to be camping out in the backyard that summer evening—to accompany him to his place of business while he closed up. As neither of us had ever been to a club (we were underage), we were thrilled to get the chance.

By the time we arrived at Joey's place, it was completely deserted of customers, but we didn't care. Joey played the jukebox for us, and my friend and I partied by ourselves, soft drinks in hand, on the darkened dance floor. Sometimes he would bring home old 45 records he had replaced in the jukebox and give them to my sister and me.

With the exception of Joey, all the rest of our neighbors were WASPs. Similar also to our old Wasena neighborhood, lots of children, including many our age, lived near our new residence. These demographic patterns typified the 1950s because of the baby boom and segregation.

We usually never had to walk more than a block to find a chum to hang out with. In our neighborhood we kids all knew each other, we democratically embraced most any kid who wanted to join our activities, and we felt safe. As usual, our parents knew where we were and what we were doing.

In one of the homes we visited often, across the street from us and one house down, lived a biology professor and his brood in a big old, rambling, white frame house. Despite our hypocritically judging the four children in that family as rather eccentric–they were introverted bookworms who tended to neglect their personal appearance—we visited back and forth with them.

The closest street running perpendicular to ours produced most of our buddies. One of my sister's dearest girlfriends, sweet, pretty Sarah, lived in an upstairs apartment in one of the houses on that street. We used to enjoy watching the cute, athletically gifted teenage boys who lived downstairs from Sarah play football on their front lawn. A couple of doors down from Sarah's, the front porch of the Perrys' provided us a great place to play canasta night after night in the summertime before many of us were old enough to secure workers' permits or to have steady sweethearts to divert us. Playing cards entertained us for untold hours on soft, warm nights.

Once in a while Pat and I or our friends would go together to see a movie. My sister and I would first try to cajole Dad into giving us a dollar (70 cents for the show, 30 cents for popcorn and a drink); but failing to squeeze blood from the proverbial turnip, we dipped into our hard-earned, meager savings from babysitting. We also had to beg transportation from a parent because none of us kids drove yet. All the movie theaters in our town, with the exceptions of the Lee Theater on Williamson Road and the Grandin in the Raleigh Court neighborhood, were located in center city Roanoke, either on Jefferson Street or Campbell Avenue. There were no theaters in malls because malls were non-existent in Roanoke in the early '50s. Downtown we had our choice of going to the American, with a fancy interior including balconies, heavy burgundy stage curtains, and large, faux gold leaf medallions emblazoning the walls; or to the Roanoke, with mediocre decor and less seating than the American; or to our least favorite, the Rialto, virtually unadorned and a little on the sleazy side.

Movies were not rated for audience suitability as they are today; they did not depict explicit sex and gory violence anyway. We liked musicals, e.g., *Seven Brides for Seven Brothers* (1954), spotlighting Howard Keel and Jane Powell, or the many others of the same genre starring Gene Kelly, Donald O'Connor, or Mitzi Gaynor. We always enjoyed the Dean Martin-Jerry Lewis comedies, such as *Sailor Beware* (1952). I particularly liked period movies, e.g., *Knights of the Round Table* (1954), featuring Robert Taylor and Ava Gardner. (In that movie, Taylor's quote as he began a military assault, "Horse to the spurs, death to the enemy" was [and is] indicative of the oft simplistic American approach to political problem solving: go charging in, destroy the bad guys de jour, [happy] end of story.)

More often than we attended movies, we watched television programs, despite the limited options of that medium in the '50s. Comedies, e.g., *Your Show of Shows* (1950-54), sparkling with Sid Caesar, Imogene Coca, and Carl Reiner, ranked among the best quality programs. Interestingly, Mel Brooks and Neil Simon, who both became household names in their own right by the 1970s and 1980s, counted among the exceptionally gifted writers for that show.[6] Some of our other favorites included the often controversial news program, Edward R. Murrow's *See it Now* (1951-57); the lively variety production called the *Toast of the Town* when it started in 1948, but in 1955 changed its name to *The Ed Sullivan Show*; a number of engrossing melodramas, such as *The Loretta Young Show* (1953-61); and the slapstick game show, *Beat the Clock* (1950-58).

Watching familiar television shows and hanging out with my newfound neighborhood friends cushioned me somewhat while I made the difficult adjustment to my permutated school milieu. We had previously lived on the more cosmopolitan, sophisticated side of town, southwest Roanoke, with a school system structured on three levels: elementary, junior high, and high school. The northwest section of Roanoke where we now lived, referred to more specifically at that time as the Williamson Road area and still perceived by many Roanokers as rough-hewn in nature, was in 1949 annexed as a part of the city. It was not until after 1960 that the Williamson Road school district adopted, due to an ever-increasing student population, a three-tiered division which wedged junior high between elementary and high schools. Prior to the '60s, elementary school ran from first through the seventh grade; high school started at the eighth grade level. As a seventh grader when we moved across town, I was demoted to elementary school where I stayed in the same classroom all day with the same teacher and pupils. At my new school Preston Park, we enjoyed no school dances, no upperclassmen to emulate (for better or worse), and no palpable sexual tension. We played games outside at recess and endured the close proximity of hundreds of giggly younger children.

Somewhat to my surprise, now regressed in elementary school, I missed the more titillating teenage atmosphere of junior high. The most venturesome action occurring in my elementary seventh grade consisted of the surreptitious circulation of what we termed "character books." If our teacher, Mrs. Richards, caught us passing one around during class, she would promptly confiscate it. (Who knows if she bothered to read our tripe.) Simply doctored up composition books, character books intimately charted the tastes and personality of one's classmates. Most of us kids owned our own character book which we would pass around for our classmates to fill out. Each person was supposed to list details about himself under the appropriate heading on each page, e.g., name, color of hair and eyes, favorite song, favorite color, favorite food, favorite movie star, ad infinitum. The manifest purpose of the book was to get to know each other better; the latent and far more important function was to ascertain who had a crush on whom or who were the most popular kids in the class. The latter could be judged from informally tallying up responses in categories such as "favorite male student in class" and "favorite female student in class." Character books at least offered a sprinkling of pubescent intrigue for me at Preston Park Elementary.[7]

Once again in elementary, I also regained my status as resident artist in my class. My teacher soon decided that I possessed a talent and often, while my classmates were slaving over their texts, let me work in the back of the room making posters or decorations for the class bulletin board.

Our end of the school year class trip to Monticello turned out to be a fun excursion too. Dressed in our finest and armed with our Brownie cameras, we embarked from school on a bus and, on our best behavior, traveled to Charlottesville (a 3-hour journey because I-81 did not exist).[8] I had never before visited the home of Jefferson, especially revered by native Virginians. Even for an unenlightened, barely 13-year-old, Monticello exuded extraordinary history inside and out, with Jefferson's innovative architecture, state-of-the-art gardens, extensive library, continental knickknacks and scientific gadgets. That outing made me feel close to being grown up, despite my elementary student status.

That same year of the big school changes, not to mention change of address, menarche arrived. Fortunately, it caught me at home. I felt something wet on my underpants, knew my bladder had not leaked, and in somewhat of a panic immediately headed for the bathroom to investigate. When I discovered blood, I thought I had inadvertently incurred a wound in a most embarrassing place. I was hesitant to approach Mama, from whom no secrets were ever long hid though, with my strange predicament. When I told her what had happened, she assured me to my surprise that it was nothing to worry about and suggested I go talk with my older sister, which I did.

When girls of my generation became women, some of us reacted with alarm and distress while others responded with pride and confidence. My friend's younger sister, for instance, comported herself as a princess when she experienced her first period. She sashayed around her house all day, expecting everybody in the family to pay due homage to her during this awesome rite of passage. Regardless of attitude or experience, one by one at this stage in life we entered the sisterhood of menstruating females, with all the attendant physiological inconveniences, the sanitary belt rating as one of the worse. Looking and feeling like yet another medieval torture device, the sanitary belt is a relatively thin elastic strap which fits snugly around the waist and stretches with loose ends down to the crotch. Metal clips on the loose ends of the strap secure the (supposed) absorbent pad while cutting into the tender skin of the lower abdomen in the front and the buttocks crack in the back. If we doubled over with excruciating menstrual cramps, some omniscient cramp-free woman or medical doctor advised us either to exercise vigorously to alleviate the pain or informed us that the pain was all in our heads.

For me, that year of the menarche constituted a red letter one for sure. After having to withstand my relegation to elementary school for the last half of the seventh grade, then having begun the aggravating monthly flow, I finally embarked upon the bittersweet journey through high school. In the fall of 1954 I started eighth grade at William Fleming High School. This was the big time. Right off I met my numerous new teachers, had to find my locker and learn the combination, pay my fees and collect all my books, and find my way around the school to my various classes as well as to the cafeteria. I had to learn to gobble my lunch in 10 minutes.

I wasn't totally unfamiliar with the student body, however, or at least I had somewhat of an orientation to names and faces through my sister. Pat, having entered Fleming the previous spring in the ninth grade, had already established a group of cronies and knew many upper classmates through participation in church activities. On a regular basis she came home from school and told me all about her chums. I hung onto her every word. Although I soon established pals my own age, I never ceased to be enamored of my sister's group and the older students, my paramount role models.

I still looked up to some of Pat's friends who had been her classmates at Woodrow but had since graduated from there to Jefferson High, our rival school across town. Pat kept up with a lot more friends than I at Jefferson because she had known them a lot longer at Woodrow. Plus, after we moved she continued to date a Jefferson boy now and then; a few even came to visit at our house on Tenth Street Extension.

A big difference between the schools I knew about on the southwest side of town—Wasena Elementary, Woodrow Wilson Junior High, and Jefferson

High—and those on the northwest side of town—Preston Park Elementary and William Fleming High—involved social class distinction. The social strata of upper, middle, and lower classes within the student population in the southwest city schools stood out much more sharply than in the Williamson Road area schools. The Roanoke City school zones incorporated students from all walks of life, rich, poor and in-between. The Williamson Road area, on the other hand, originally drew citizenry who preferred to live outside the city or who were less inclined to be status seekers or to worry about living at the right address. If they had entertained such notions, they would've sought residence in the more upper-class sections of Roanoke City. Consequently, most of the students in northwest schools hailed from less social conscious, middle-class or blue collar families, and the atmosphere was much more egalitarian than in southwest Roanoke. Granted, the middle class students could be divided socially and economically into gradations: lower-, middle-, and upper-middle class. But the student bodies of both Preston Park and Fleming barely discerned or seemed to care about class divisions.

Social class issues notwithstanding, excitement in high school centered around football. As one might imagine, fierce school rivalry prevailed, especially in sports, between the huge, more wealthy, more urbane Jefferson High and the much smaller populated, less cosmopolitan upstart, Fleming High. Lest one forget, Jefferson High is the namesake of our illustrious third president while our bush-league high school was named after a mere Scottish medical doctor, Colonel Fleming, who fought Indians in the United States before the Revolutionary War. (Fleming died and is actually buried in the Williamson Road vicinity of Roanoke.)[9]

Downtown Victory Stadium, the game site for all the home football games of both high schools, was always packed for the annual Jefferson-Fleming blood feud game.[10] Emotions ran high, with the usual deeply insulting or condescending remarks flying back and forth from adversarial sides of the stadium. Since I knew little or nothing about the actual game of football, I didn't pay much attention to the game itself. Nonetheless, I passionately enjoyed being there, getting caught up in the boisterous crowd's enthusiasm. Aside from the adrenaline surge, the mild, beautiful autumn evenings, the exceptionally cute, vivacious cheerleaders (I was a wanna be), and the newly purchased, good-looking fall clothes I wore at the games, all added up to a glorious time. Once in a while I would truly zone in on the field action to watch a particular football player if one of my friends or I happened to have a crush on him.

My most favorite activity associated with football, of course, was the sock hop held in our school gym after every home game. I happened to be a dancing fool, and besides, hops equated with romance and popular music–the stuff teenage dreams are made of. In the eighth grade none of us was old enough to drive and hence park and make out, so a dance position offered the only socially acceptable way to cling to the object of our affection.

In addition to the new world of football, parties became part of the high school scene for me. Not like the birthday parties we elementary school children attended where our most wanton behavior amounted to playing spin the bottle and stealing kisses in broad daylight in front of Mom and twenty kids, these social gatherings seriously thrilled us hormone-driven adolescents. We definitely felt sexual arousals but had little idea what to do with them. Besides which, our families, and all the rest of the major social institutions, bound us to chastity upon pain of disgrace, banishment, damnation and hell. Add to these prohibitions our pandemic teenage self-consciousness and one can understand our inhibitions towards members of the opposite sex. With all these strikes against us, at our eighth grade coed parties, typically held in a dimly lit basement recreation room, the boys invariably milled around on one side of the room while the girls stood on the other side of the room watching the boys mill. Once in a while the two genders would meet at the chips and dip bowl, where if one lucked out, fingers touched going after the same chip. As the evening wore on, if the boys never braved asking the girls to dance, girls resorted to dancing with each other.

Despite all this electric boy-girl excitement in the eighth grade, I persevered in some of my more sedate activities such as reading and studying. Mom drilled into us kids from an early age the standard middle-class dictates: you must study, you must acquire a good education, you must achieve good grades, you must be obedient, you must be a good girl (translation: if you get pregnant before marriage, you might as well kill yourself). So along with some very intrepid, faddish friends, I retained comparatively more serious ones who shared my interest in scholastics. One of my more intellectual, closest friends in the eighth grade was Mary Ann, who happened to live within easy walking distance of my home. She and I throughly enjoyed sleeping over at her house (she was an only child, so we didn't have to put up with pesky siblings), reading ourselves to sleep. To obtain books, we adventurously hopped on a city bus and rode downtown to the city library. We usually got off one block from our destination along Jefferson Street so we could first treat ourselves to a few delectable chocolates from the Martha Washington Candy Store.

One book in particular (alas, I cannot find the title) Mary Ann checked out and read me passages from stands out in my mind. It was a sci-fi story about how a group of pacifists managed to capture a superbomb capable of blowing up the entire planet, and then forced world peace on everybody by threatening to detonate the bomb if anybody initiated hostilities. Given our "age of anxiety" over nuclear destruction, that story somehow gave Mary Ann and me hope.

One evening at Mary Ann's turned out to be a far cry from our usual relatively staid ones. She and some other friends all belonged to a sorority (we had several at Fleming, none of which were legitimized by our school) which they invited me to join. Upon my acceptance, the sorority carried out a particularly onerous part of initiation for me one evening at Mary Ann's house. They compelled me to eat a garbage sandwich—a nasty mishmash of cold, slimy, cooked spinach, mashed potatoes, and catsup on white loaf bread— washed down by a raw egg. After prodigious gagging, I never felt quite the same about staying over at Mary Ann's.

Initiation into a sorority at our high school characteristically required paying membership dues of $5 per year and making oneself look as ugly as possible (the height of non-femininity in our minds and therefore signifying a huge sacrifice) at school for a week or so. Appearing at our worst entailed dressing in a homely, unbecoming fashion; wearing a stupid hair-do and no lipstick; and obeying every command, no matter how ridiculous, of our sorority sisters. We expertly and assiduously hid from our boyfriends so as not to repulse them.

Being so self-absorbed with our sororities, crushes on boys, football games, parties, self-identities, and even school work, we were barely conscious of what was going on outside our circumscribed, parochial, pubescent world. About the only forums in school on social issues occurred in Mr. Barber's science class. Mr. Barber, also a truant officer but nonetheless beloved by us, was attuned to adolescent needs and problems. In his class, we sometimes talked about some relatively trivial matters, such as whether teenage girls should wear make-up, and if so, how much. But we also addressed much more significant subjects like school integration. In 1955 Rosa Parks refused to give up her seat on the bus in Montgomery, Alabama. We knew that the segregated world we had grown up in would not (and should not, in a great many of our southern minds) hold. Concerned that our school activities, my beloved sock hops, for example, would be curtailed with integration, we frequently steered Mr. Barber in the direction of that hot topic. From his responses on the subject, I distinctly sensed that our esteemed teacher objected to integration of schools, or at the least, the problems he believed it would pose. He may have shared the inordinate fear many of the adults in our cosmos harbored of interracial marriages, which they perceived as the ultimate outcome of integrated schools. We kids didn't worry much about miscegenation or interracial liaisons; instead, prospects of prohibited social activities, however generated, perturbed us infinitely more.

Nevertheless, we eighth graders in touching upon the issues of school desegregation and changes in the relationship between the sexes, not to mention the threat of nuclear conflagration, were becoming initiated into a brave new world. Unbeknownst to us, we presaged the cusp of the 1960s when horrendous political upheavals, military quagmire, and social schisms and conflict over inequalities and injustices of all sorts loomed just over the horizon.

NOTES

1. Bill Haley and his Comets made a huge hit with us before we ever heard of Elvis Presley. Although Elvis cut his first official record in 1954, with "That's All Right Mama" on one side and "Blue Moon of Kentucky" on the flip side, our crowd didn't discover this future "King" of rock n' roll until 1955. Rollin, 181.

2. Hurricane Hazel hit the United States at Wilmington, N.C., but its enormous forward speed caused great damage much further inland, traveling as far north as Canada. In Virginia communities Hazel toppled trees and caused flooding.

3. This was the fourth time in the ten years between 1945 and 1955 that my family had changed residences, not unusual though, given the high mobility of Americans.

4. Our crowd didn't frequent Toot's because of its notoriety for harboring a "wild" clientele, i.e., the supposedly hard core teenage rebels who drove souped-up, drag racing cars or who smoked and drank. Our mild-mannered bunch most often hung out at Gill's Restaurant on Williamson Road. It didn't offer curbside service; we had to park, go inside, vie for an empty booth and then order their minuscule (by today's standards) but fabulous tasting, fresh, juicy burgers.

5. Contrarily, I fervently wished for all night radio and t.v. broadcasts when school was not in session and before I started dating or working. Often times my brain circuitry refused to shut down late at night, with nothing for entertainment but my own worrisome thoughts.

6. O'Neill, 79.

7. I dare say, our character books of the 1950s were the forerunners of today's online "Facebook" for high schools as well as for some universities and other organizations.

8. A field trip called for wearing our nicest clothes. As was the case for any special occasion in the 1950s, children dressed up. Adults in similar circumstances donned their best too. Men wore suits, ties and hats while women wore dresses, high heels, hats, and gloves, not to mention perfectly coiffed hair.

9. Virginia Writers' Project, 48.

10. From 1900 until 1971 Victory Stadium also hosted the annual Thanksgiving Day Football Classic between VMI (Virginia Military Institute) and VPI (Virginia Polytechnic Institute, now more nationally known as Virginia Tech). Local merchants happily supported the event because out-of-town fans stayed over and inaugurated their Christmas shopping in downtown Roanoke.

SUGGESTED READINGS

Breines, Wini. *Young, White, and Miserable: Growing Up Female in the Fifties.* Boston: Beacon Press, 1992.

Castleman, Harry and Walter Podrazik. *Watching TV: Four Decades of American Television.* New York: McGraw-Hill, 1982.

Conant, James B. *The American High School Today.* New York: McGraw-Hill, 1959.

Goldman, Eric. *The Crucial Decade: America 1945-1955.* New York: Knopf, 1956.

Halberstam, David. *The Fifties.* New York: Villard Books, 1993.

Miller, Douglas T., and Marion Nowak. *The Fifties: The Way We Really Were.* New York: Doubleday, 1977.

O'Neill, William L. *American High: The Years of Confidence, 1945-1960.* New York: The Free Press, 1986.

Prillaman, Helen R. *A Place Apart: A Brief History of the Early Williamson Road and North Roanoke Valley Residents and Places.* Baltimore, Md.: Genealogical Publishing Co., 1997.

Rollin, Lucy. *Twentieth-Century Teen Culture by the Decades.* Westport, Conn.: Greenwood Press, 1999.

Virginia Writers' Project. *Roanoke: Story of County and City.* Roanoke, Va.: Stone Printing Co., 1942.

Epilogue

Embarking upon new horizons, we were learning that our generation did not always view issues in the same light as did our parents, that change is inevitable, and that sides in moral dilemmas are not always black and white. ' Thirteen years old and in the eighth grade in 1955, my friends and I straddled two worlds: the childhood we were trying to shed and the adulthood that would take us years to attain. Physical changes put our bodies at odds with ourselves. We were clumsy, outgrowing our ill-fitting clothes, we females taller than many of our male cohorts, most all of us unsure of who we were as individuals and how we should behave. Our interest in the opposite sex so absorbed our psyches that most of us spent little mental energy on news headlines or any serious subjects outside our limited teenage universe. If and when we did contemplate politics or world affairs, it usually left us feeling depressed or fearful. The aggression of the Soviet Union, the arms race, and the threat of a nuclear attack seemed to us gargantuan, insurmountable problems.

Always an apprehensive child, I found adolescence to be no more serene. I had not traveled far in the decade spanning the middle of the twentieth century, yet changes inside and outside my private life proliferated. Spending my earliest years in a little backwater community in the Appalachian region of North Carolina amidst large extended families on both my mother's and father's sides, I fretted over my mother's state of health, my grandmother Miller's malevolent deities, hurtful playmates, and a school much too huge for my insecure, physically tiny person.

I spent the next five years in another small southern community, Roanoke, in the Blue Ridge Mountains of Virginia. Within that five years my family lived in three different residences and I attended three different schools. My fears over Mama's health were not assuaged during that entire period. What's more, I agonized over my own health, tormented by the possibility of having my leg amputated. My closest elementary school friends no longer desired my companionship after we entered junior high school, from junior high I had to revert back to an elementary school setting, and from there I had to adjust to an abrupt transition from an elementary to a high school environment. All these permutations produced nail-biting (literally) but positive excitement as well.

But mine was not the only life undergoing metamorphosis: by 1955 a different America was emerging. In just the year before, McCarthy was censured by his senate colleagues, the Supreme Court ruled against segregation in public schools in *Brown v. Board of Education of Topeka* and Eisenhower proposed an Interstate Highway System. In 1955, President Eisenhower held his first televised press conference, and, since the French had pulled out of Indochina, the U.S. Government started sending aid to Southeast Asia. All these events portended immense social and cultural change in our country.

The values and beliefs that our parents and the major institutions of our society had inculcated in us would both sustain us and be challenged in the future. For the most part, we lower-middle and middle-class, young Caucasians in mid-twentieth century trusted God, our government, American corporations, and the media. Steeped in the Protestant Ethic, honest and hard-working, we showed respect for our elders. From childhood we fully believed that education is the key to success, that advanced technology is always good and that any individual can work his or her way to the top of the social and economic ladder if s/he really tries hard enough. We naively gave credence to the American dream of progress for everything and everybody.

For my peers and me and for American society in general, the obliviousness to social groups different from us, provincialism, the innocent persona, and the acceptance of the status quo were beginning to slip away. In another five years many of us would be in college, while others would ship out to a war in Southeast Asia. Still others would be raising their own families. We could not have imagined what the '60s decade of our lives would bring: the Vietnam War, the Anti-War Movement, the Women's Liberation Movement, backlash to the Civil Rights Movement, the Black Liberation Movement, the Hippy Movement, the Generation Gap, the Beatles ushering in whole new genres of music (not to mention hairstyles), Woodstock, John F. Kennedy's Camelot and tragic death, and the Cuban missile crisis which many believed would trigger the long-feared nuclear holocaust.

The best and the worst were yet to come.

Bibliography

Ahlstrom, Sydney E. *A Religious History of the American People*. New Haven, Conn.: Yale UP, 1972.

Anderson, J. Jay. *North Wilkesboro: The First 100 Years, 1890-1990*. Charlotte, N.C.: Delmar Co., 1990.

Barfield, Ray. *Listening to Radio*. Westport, Conn.: Praeger, 1996.

Barnes, Raymond P. *A History of Roanoke*. Radford, Va.: Commonwealth Press, 1968.

Barson, Michael. *"Better Dead Than Red": A Nostalgic Look at the Golden Years of Russiaphobia, Red-Baiting, and Other Commie Madness*. New York: Hyperion, 1992.

Blair, Clay. *The Forgotten War: America in Korea, 1950-1953*. New York: Times Books, 1987.

Borio, Gene. "The History of Tobacco Part III." www.historian.org/bysubject/tobacco3.htm. (4 Feb. 2006)

Boyer, Paul. *By the Bomb's Early Light: American Thought and Culture at the Dawn of the Atomic Age*. New York: Pantheon, 1985.

Breines, Wini. *Young, White, and Miserable: Growing Up Female in the Fifties*. Boston: Beacon Press, 1992.

Brown, JoAnne. "'A is for Atom, B is for Bomb': Civil Defense in American Public Education, 1948-1963." *Journal of American History* 75, no. 1 (June 1988): 68-90.

Bryant, Jessie Bunker. *The Connected Bunkers*. Winston-Salem: J.B. Bunker, 2001.

Castleman, Harry, and Walter Podrazik. *Watching TV: Four Decades of American Television*. New York: Praeger, 1984.

Caute, David. *The Great Fear: The Anti-Communist Purge Under Truman and Eisenhower*. New York: Simon & Schuster, 1978.

Conant, James B. *The American High School Today*. New York: McGraw-Hill, 1959.

Crews, C. Daniel, and Richard W. Starbuck. *With Courage for the Future: The Story of the Moravian Church, Southern Province*. Winston-Salem: Blair Publishing, 2002.

Davis, J. Lee. *Bits of History and Legends Around and about the Natural Bridge of Virginia, from 1730 to 1950*. Lynchburg, Va.: Natural Bridge of Virginia, Inc., 1949.

Davis, Stephen. *Say, Kids! What Time is it? Notes from the Peanut Gallery*. Boston: Little, Brown, and Co., 1987.

Doherty, Thomas Patrick. *Cold War, Cool Medium: Television, McCarthyism, and American Culture*. New York: Columbia UP, 2003.

Donovan, Robert J. *Conflict and Crisis: The Presidency of Harry S. Truman, 1945-1948*. New York: Norton, 1972.

———. *Tumultuous Years: The Presidency of Harry S. Truman, 1949-1953*. New York: Norton, 1982.

Dreger, Alice Domurat. *One of Us: Conjoined Twins and the Future of Normal*. Cambridge, Mass.: Harvard UP, 2004.

Ellison, Ralph. *Invisible Man*. New York: Random House, 1952.

Fried, Richard M. *Nightmare in Red: The McCarthy Era in Perspective*. Oxford, N.Y.: Oxford UP, 1990.

Gately, Iain. *Tobacco: A Cultural History of how an Exotic Plant Seduced Civilization*. New York: Grove Press, 2001.

Gillon, Steve M. *Boomer Nation: The Largest and Richest Generation Ever and How it Changed America*. New York: The Free Press, 2004.

Goldman, Eric. *The Crucial Decade: America 1945-1955*. New York: Knopf, 1956.

Goodman, Jordan. *Tobacco in History and Culture*. Detroit: Charles Scribner's Sons, 2004.

———. *Tobacco in History: The Cultures of Dependence*. London: Routledge, 1993.

Goulden, Joseph C. *The Best Years–1945-1950*. New York: Atheneum, 1976.

Graebner, William. *The Age of Doubt: American Thought and Culture in the 1940s*. Boston: Twayne Pub., 1991.

Grossman, James K. *Black Southerners and the Great Migration*. Chicago: University of Chicago Press, 1989.

Halberstam, David. *The Fifties*. New York: Villard Books, 1993.

Haralovich, MaryBeth and Lawin Rabinovitz, eds. *Television, History, and American Culture*. Durham, N.C.: Duke UP, 1999.

Harrell, David Edwin, Jr. *Oral Roberts: An American Life*. Bloomington, Ind.: Indiana UP 1985.

Hart, John Fraser. *The Changing Scale of American Agriculture*. Charlottesville, Va.: University of Virginia Press, 2003.

Hartmann, Susan M. *The Home Front and Beyond: American Women in the 1940s*. Boston: Twayne Pub., 1982.

Hastings, Max. *The Korean War*. New York: Simon & Schuster, 1987.

Henriksen, Margot A. *Dr. Strangelove's America: Society and Culture in the Atomic Age*. Berkeley: University of California Press, 1997.

Higgins, Tom, and Steve Waid. *Junior Johnson: Brave in Life*. Phoenix: David Bull Pub., 1999.

Hoover, J. Edgar. *Masters of Deceit: The Story of Communism in America and How to Fight It*. New York: Henry Holt, 1958.

Hornsby, Alton. *Chronology of African-American History from 1942 to the Present*. 2nd ed. Detroit: Gale Research, 1997.

Howell, Mark D. *From Moonshine to Madison Avenue: A Cultural History of the NASCAR Winston Cup Series*. Bowling Green, O.: Bowling Green State University Popular Press, 1997.

Irving, David. *Goring: A Bibliography*. New York: Morrow, 1989.

Jack, George S., and Edward Boyle Jacobs. *History of Roanoke County*. Roanoke, Va.: Stone Printing Co., 1912.

Jacobs, E.B. *History of Roanoke City and History of the Norfolk and Western Railway Co*. Roanoke, Va.: Stone Printing Co., 1912.

Jenkins, Garry. "Wind Energy–A Brief History and Current Status." *Nutrition and Food Science* (March 1999):157.

Kaledin, Eugenia. *American Women in the 1950s: Mothers and More*. Boston: Twayne Pub., 1984.

——. *Daily Life in the United States, 1940-1959*. Shifting Worlds. Westport, Conn.: Greenwood Press, 2000.

Kay, Patty. "Whatever Happened to North Wilkesboro." http://www.insiderracingnews .com. (12 Apr. 2003).

Kluger, Jeffrey. *Splendid Solution: Jonas Salk and the Conquest of Polio*. New York: G. P. Putnam's Sons, 2004.

Lambie, Joseph T. *From Mine to Market: The History of Coal Transportation on the Norfolk and Western Railway*. New York: New York UP, 1954.

Larkin, David. *Mill: The History and Future of Naturally Powered Buildings*. New York: Universe Pub., 2000.

Laurence, William L. *The Hell Bomb*. New York: Knopf, 1951.

Layman, Richard, ed. *American Decades: 1950-1959*. Detroit: Gale Research, 1994.

Leffland, Ella. *The Knight, Death and the Devil*. New York: Morrow, 1990.

Manchester, William Raymond. *American Caesar: Douglas MacArthur*. Boston: Little, Brown, 1978.

Margolick, David. *Beyond Glory: Joe Louis vs. Max Schmeling, and a World on the Brink*. New York: Knopf, 2005.

Marling, Karal Ann. *As Seen on TV: The Visual Culture of Everyday Life in the 1950s*. Cambridge, Mass.: Harvard UP, 1994.

Miller, Douglas T., and Marion Nowak. *The Fifties: The Way We Really Were*. New York: Doubleday, 1977.

Mohlenbrock, Robert H. "Mt. Rogers, Virginia (Jefferson National Forest)." *Natural History* vol. 11 (Dec. 1990): 72-73.

Morris, T. N. "Management and Preservation of Food." Pp. 26-52 in *A History of Technology*, ed. by C. Singer et al. Vol. 5. Oxford: Clarendon, 1958.

Moss, Norman. *Men Who Play God: The Story of the H-Bomb and How the World Came to Live With It*. New York: Harper and Rowe, 1968.

Nathan, Joan. "Red, White, and Blueberry." *U. S. New & World Report* (15/22 Aug. 2005): 71.

The Natural Bridge: An Ancient Natural Wonder in Virginia's Shenandoah Valley. Historic Landmark and Nature Park, Caverns, Monacan Indian Village, Hotel. Natural Bridge, Va.: Natural Bridge of Virginia, 2005.

Noll, Mark A. *A History of Christianity in the United States and Canada*. Grand Rapids, Mich.: William B. Eerdmans Pub. Co., 1992.

Bibliography

O'Neill, William L. *American High: Confident Years* 1945-1960. New York: The Free Press, 1986.

Oshinsky, David M. *Polio: An American Story.* Oxford, N.Y.: Oxford UP, 2005.

Patterson, James T. *Grand Expectations: The United States, 1945-1974.* Oxford, N.Y.: Oxford UP, 1996.

Prillaman, Helen R. *A Place Apart: A Brief History of the Early Williamson Road and North Roanoke Valley Residents and Places.* Baltimore, Md.: Genealogical Pub. Co., 1997.

Ridgway, Matthew. *The Korean War.* New York: Doubleday & Co., 1967.

Rollin, Lucy. *Twentieth Century Teen Culture by the Decades.* Westport, Conn.: Greenwood Press, 1999.

Rose, Lisle Abbott. *Cold War Comes to Main Street: America in 1950.* Lawrence, Kan.: University Press of Kansas, 1999.

Satin, Joseph, ed. *The 1950's: America's "Placid" Decade.* Boston: Houghton Mifflin, 1960.

Schlebecker, John T. *Whereby We Thrive: A History of American Farming, 1607-1972.* Ames, Ia.: Iowa State University Press, 1975.

Schlesinger, Arthur M., ed. *The Almanac of American History.* New York: Barnes & Noble Books, 2004.

Seavey, Nina Gilden, Jane S. Smith, and Paul Wagner. *A Paralyzing Fear: The Triumph over Polio in America.* New York: TV Books, 1989.

Shephard, Sue. *Pickled, Potted, and Canned.* New York: Simon & Schuster, 2000.

Slaughter, Thomas P. *The Whiskey Rebellion: Frontier Epilogue to the American Revolution.* Oxford, N.Y.: Oxford UP, 1986.

Smith, Robert. *MacArthur in Korea.* New York: Simon & Schuster, 1982.

Spock, Benjamin. *The Commonsense Book of Baby and Child Care.* New York: Duell, Sloan and Pearce, 1946.

Striplin, E. F. Pat. *The Norfolk and Western: A History.* Forest, Va.: Norfolk & Western Historical Society, 1997.

"That's Racin'." *Charlotte Observer,* 9 Oct. 1999.

Thorne, Stuart. *The History of Food Preservation.* Kirby Lonsdale, Cumbria, England: Parthenon, 1986.

Tursi, Frank V. *Winston-Salem: A History.* Winston-Salem: Blair Publishing, 1994.

Underwood, Dick. "A Brief History of North Wilkesboro." www.northwilkesboro.com/history. (9 Feb. 2006).

Viens, Nicholas A. *Antibiotic Reactions: The Changing Faces of Disease and Medicine in America Before and After Penicillin.* Dissertation, 2003.

Virginia Writers' Project. *Roanoke: Story of County and City.* Roanoke, Va.: Stone Printing Co., 1942.

Wallace, Irving and Amy. *The Two: A Biography.* New York: Simon and Schuster, 1978.

Walls, Dwayne E. *The Chickenbone Special.* New York: Harcourt Brace Jovanovich, Inc., 1971.

Weart, Spencer R. *Nuclear Fear: A History of Images.* Cambridge, Mass.: Harvard UP, 1988.

Webb, James. *Born Fighting*. New York: Broadway Books, 2004.

White, Clare. *Roanoke 1740-1982*. Roanoke, Va.: Hickory Printing, 1982.

Wise, Suzanne. *From Moonshine to Merlot: The History of North Wilkesboro Speedway as a Reflection of the Growth of NASCAR*. Boone, N.C.: S. Wise, 2004.

Witwer, David Scott. *Corruption and Reform in the Teamsters Union*. Urbana, Ill.: University of Illinois Press, 2003.

www.greeneggsandsam.com/eastbend. (23 Jan. 2006).

Index